Discovering

Gerald Middents

DISCOVERING

iUniverse books may be ordered through booksellers or by contacting:

iUniverse
1663 Liberty Drive
Bloomington, IN 47403
www.iuniverse.com
844-349-9409

Because of the dynamic nature of the Internet, any web addresses or links contained in this book may have changed since publication and may no longer be valid. The views expressed in this work are solely those of the author and do not necessarily reflect the views of the publisher, and the publisher hereby disclaims any responsibility for them.

Any people depicted in stock imagery provided by Getty Images are models, and such images are being used for illustrative purposes only. Certain stock imagery © Getty Images.

ISBN: 978-1-6632-4602-8 (sc)
ISBN: 978-1-6632-4603-5 (e)

Print information available on the last page.

iUniverse rev. date: 12/30/2022

CONTENTS

FATHOMING

What can do we about fathoming?
It is related to understanding.
We need to do some probing!
In the process of defining.

This becomes a depth process;
Fathoming requires us to digest.
Our brains may do this exploring;
In these procedures for learning.

We engage our brains in discovering;
This is demanded in our fathoming.
We engage in this as exciting;
Our lives will be growing.

Depth requires our fathoming,
Parallel to deep water swimming.
Our brain will also require probing,
Similar to processes of composing!

Our brains will engage in stretching;
Even without our own knowing.
Now let us do our preparing;
In processes of expanding.

Yes, we will be "participling!"
With this new word we are using.
Participles are also very exciting;
Others may see this as stretching.

This is composed in poetry!
What you write is worthy.
Each line has meaning;
We are now composing.

Use time to contemplate;
Some ideas arise very late.
Have fun in your thinking;
Enjoy while you are writing.

PROBING

Yes, let us engage in deep probing;
This is a key strategy in composing.
It is time to engage in deepening;
In deep water, we are swimming!

We are not naturally like fish;
And fish are not at all like us!
We can learn from each other;
Fish could be our sister or brother!

Fish can help us to swim deeper!
We learn to become breathers.
This takes deep fathoming;
With fish, this is the thing.

We can teach fish to sing!!
It is for more than swimming.
Like us "SWIMMING in the RAIN,"
We all benefit as jointly we gain.

DISCOVERING

A. HUMAN CURIOSITY:

Humanity has special roles on Earth;
We can help to discover our worth.
We are blessed upon this planet
Discovery is for our own benefit.

We are also active in exploring;
To find planets who do encircling!
To locate them is very exciting;
The key process is worth printing.

Maybe it does have living creatures;
Magazines create articles as features!
Investigators value explorations
As scientists hope for publications.

The Universe has many planets;
Explorers consider them magnets.
When will they be discovered?
Will ingredients be uncovered?

Exploration takes determination;
Unable to stop at a station.
Researchers go forward;
Investigations go onward.

Much exploration requires traveling;
By air, by sea or by walking.
Or also by quality imagining.[1]
These methods al take financing.

---

[1] Middents, G., 2022, IMAGINING, iUniverse, Bloomington, Indiana, USA.

Every day, we are discovering;
This Universe, our home for living!
New experiences this Earth is providing;
We know a part of what is existing.

As humans, we have limitations;
Just a small slice of creation.
This piece is on our awareness;
Unfolding in our consciousness.

This Universe is very expansive;
Our minds hopefully are intensive!
How far does our Universe extend?
Where did it begin? How far expand?

Our questions are very important;
Our minds hope to be significant!
Let us make our contributions!
As we try to explore inventions.

Realize that we can do discovering;
These mysteries await uncovering!
These processes can be pursued;
As humanity searches for clues.

WHAT DO YOU WANT?

Do you want possessions or relations?
Are these desires tangible or intangible?
Possible answers now are to be considered!
As these quantities and qualities are delivered!
The following contrasts will clarify each one
To help you how your preferences have begun!

Tangible things include seas and land
Plus, the skies and clouds plus valleys!
Intangibles are often about relationships!
Including friends and people in partnerships!
Now things you may place your hands upon,
While relations are not physical phenomena!

You can see icecaps as clear possibilities!
But you more likely would feel forgiveness!
Mountaintops challenge us to conquest!
Love is an internal emotion than a touch!
We need water and food to survive
While hopeful purpose peps us to live!

Consider the sun, planets and moons!
These are real places in our universe!
In contrast, caring love is invisible!
We may feel these as intangible!
These are essentials in order to exist
So human life will be able to persist!

WHAT ARE OUR CONTRIBUTIONS?

Helping is primarily an intangible quality!
Assisting us to maintain being healthy!
Shown by people and things for livelihood!
Another quality involves being understood!
But plants, grains, fish even our water
Are physical sources for which we barter!

Consider rain, snow and ice in different seasons
These are combinations of H2O chemicals!
Most tangible things we may be called stuff!
Often, we make stuff than what is needed!
These are treasured while we live on earth
But in our dying, what is all this but stuff!

Upon death, intangible qualities are valued!
Gracious love and forgiveness are worthwhile!
Heaven is considered as being with our God!
This relationship is intangible for us to hold!
We rely on tangible terms to be concrete,
But intangibly heaven is where we meet!

These intangibles help provide us meaning
Described primarily for us as fulfilling!
Purpose is powerful in our own living
Plus, destiny is reason for our existing!
We can also be connecting and holding
Listening may as important as talking!

Appreciating applies to all relating and things!
While Intangibles include "I-THOU" relating!
These become valuable extraordinary experiences!
Sustaining us to dream and become envisioning!
Our temptation is wanting and valuing all of these!
In exploring life's peaks of conscious "aware-nesses!"

ENDLESS POSSIBILITIES

Do we think for here and now in time and space?
Could we exist without ancestors and Divinity?
Are we on our own without any purposefulness?
What further reasons provide us with hopefulness?
These are questions that have defining destiny!
What will we contribute to our future posterity?

Questions probe and stimulate our thinking!
Whatever could be our purposeful meaning?
Why is our conscious awareness ever designed?
We build on past accumulation of awareness!
Do we give value to intangibles and tangibles?
What are visible things and invisible qualities?

Current and future purpose involves teleology!
Combining reasons for now and futurology!
Purposive meaningfulness can be our legacy!
Building on our past to be left for posterity!
Rationales for existence challenge us currently!
Plus realizing that what we do is an opportunity!

These verses are designed to become challenging!
Plus realizing we have limits in our answering!
Adding to the "scaffold" of human exploring;
Hopefully confronts for being contributing!
Active involvements invite your creating
Additional avenues for future human living!

B. SCOPE:

WHO???
HOW???
WHY???
WHERE?
WHEN??

The Early Humans lived in Africa;
Then traveled to Aisa and Australia.
Then to Europe and the Americas!
They certainly were adventurers.

Humans learned processes of discovering
We benefit from pathways of learning.
This exploration is very important,
So, we should not be reluctant.

Of course, there are risks involved;
We learn how problems are solved.
Our own experiences do build up,
These problems are step by step.

We do find meaning in living;[2]
A helpful basis is in family living!
Each family member is important.
Special meaning to parents and siblings.

Another basis is our work and career;
Meaningful labor does become clear.

---

[2] Shemer, M., 2018, "Heaven on Earth: The Scientific Search for the Afterlife, Immortality and Utopia, Henry Holt and Company, New York.

We invest our energy into our work;
This demands we be sharp and alert.

Meaning is found in transcendent spirituality;
Prompts our hope for personal immortality.
Yes, these aspirations are very powerful;
Many acknowledge living is spiritual.

Our involvements typically are interpersonal,
Interacting so that we expand our world.
This includes social-political involvements;
As we value the power of our government.

Yes, there are major challenges in living;
As a consequence, we discover meaning!
We are blessed as our lives are exciting!
Therefore, humans enjoy discovering!

DISCOVER YOUR INNER "Self!"

Who is this being called "SELF?"
Who shows up with quiet stealthy!
Appearing for essence and existence
Is this "Self" also multi-dimensional?

Self shows up without and within!
Expansively in depth and breadth!
Self also has width and breadth!
Plus traveling from past to present!

Examples may help to consider
"Myself" refers to internal person!
"Yourself" refers to you presently
"Themselves" connotes outsiders!

Psychoanalyst Carl Jung's "self" [3]
To integrate one's shadow and persona!
Webster's Dictionary has 400 references
Such as "self-worth" and "self-hood!

Maslow featured "self-actualization!" [4]
A person's need to signify interaction!
Rogers' self suggests one's internal reference, [5]
To refer to one's own personal preference!

Self is like an internal being!
A guiding balance for coping!
Does "self" relate to one's soul?
Concept describing one's whole!

PERSONHOOD

Personhood refers to legal agency
Defining a person's responsibility!
When does a child enter personhood?
Varies among abortionist's livelihood!

How does a child develop "self?"
With awareness as distinctive?
Beyond its Mother as a person?
Conscious of one's self-hood?

Do animals develop a "self?"
Few see in a mirror themself!
Research is essential for essence!
For a living creature's existence!

---

[3] Jung, C., 2014, <u>COLLECTED WORKS,</u> Princeton University Press.

[4] Maslow, A.,

[5] Rogers,

At times humans have difficulties
With limited human faculties.
Our cognition has limited range,
Small sounds may be strange.

Animals may see better than we;
As dogs have broad sensitivity.
Fish have very good eyesight;
They can see day and night!

CONNECTIONS

How do self and mind connect?
Is self both physical and mental?
Is "self" an all-inclusive term?
Including mental and spiritual?

Key items arise about meaning!
Is meaning central in one's living?
Is meaning understood by others?
Valued by sisters and brothers?

Is self the seat of consciousness?
Including ideas of self-awareness?
These issues challenge more research!
To clarify rather than leave in a lurch!
They may detect small movements,
For small change as significant.

"SELFIES!"

Selfies are widely shared today!
Photos without words to say

Many are with special people
A message that both are equal?

Yes, facial expressions communicate!
Reading eyes frequently celebrate!
The happy faces pose a few seconds,
After selfies, then what happens?

Are these efforts to discover more?
Like your own inner "self?" to adore?
Could this also be your smaller self?
Waiting to be revealed as yourself?

Selfies may we waiting to emerge!
To reveal your own hidden surge?
Secrets hidden may hope to show
You are complex in order to know!

Most selfies flash by very rapidly!
Actual "selves" exist indefinitely!
Do "selfies" show life in transitory?
"Moment by Moment" for continuity?

This age is dominated by technology!
Life on fast track that occurs quickly!
Photos capture key moments in lives!
Speeding by but not found in archives!

DISCOVERING the UNIVERSE

Discovering is a life-time process;
This challenges all living creatures.
Humans are exploring the Universe.

Yes, this Universe is very vast,
For billions of years, it is cast!
We try to investigate its expanse.

Yes, we are blessed with curiosity;
At time, we may find this risky!
But we will risk our safety.

The Early Humans lived in Africa;
Then traveled to Aisas and Australia.
Then to Europe and the Americas!

Judeo-Christian Faith in the Middle East,
Cultivated love, faith and also peace.
These qualities often put to a test!

Yes, we are now called to share these;
Even in times that are also very risky!
What would life be like without discovery?

6

HUMAN CREATIVITY

Creativity already has many explorations
"Stress Prompts Humans to Constructive Action!"
Early evidence reveals reactions!
Coping with difficult calculations
With mastery of original creations.

Early human erectus was confronted
With dangerous challenges that prompted!
Their efforts to cope with nature
They were fascinated with fire!
Creative mastery to then acquire!

6 Ferrara, Silvia, 2021, <u>What would life be without discovering?</u>

Naturally they observed lightening
In fact, it was very likely frightening!
Lightening was among many fears!
Like spontaneous fires would occur
Their curiosity continued to grow!

Likely, they corralled natural fires
It permitted them become inspired!
Efforts to keep fires to be ongoing
They discovered limits in raining.
This prompted further discovering!

FROM FLINTING TO COOKING

Crashing flint rocks for sparks,
These experiments had results!
With dry material they could ignite
Small flames to glow in the night!
This discovery they could apply!

Cooking raw food soon happened,
Thus, their protein was increased!
The human brain thereafter grew!
Advancing more problem-solving
So that they could go on creating!

Raw meat is difficult for digestion!
Green vegetables cook for ingestion!
Human bodies then became stronger!
Permitting migrations even further!
Moreover, creativity could wonder!

The ingenuity of fire and cooking
Strengthened human problem-solving!
New inventions included many tools

They would not be found by fools!
Growing bodies and brains evolved!

STORY-TELLING

Ancient languages permitted stories,
At night around the fire about glories!
Fire inspires humans to gather round!
The quiet of night invited their sounds,
Unable to hunt to gather for their foods!

Story-telling conveyed many myths
As cultures developed their histories.
Moreover, this encouraged languages
New generations knew about sages!
Stories expanded into many tales!

Languages multiplied their intelligence
Building on early discoveries to advance!
Additional creativity gave humans a chance.
So, humans developed more awareness!
Consciousness enlarged human insights!

With portability, humans adventured
Out to new locations they ventured!
The Old World populated progressively!
The New World had humans eventually!
Populating much of the world globally!

While fire can be very dangerous
Humans learned how to contain it!
These advancements had implications!
Fire could be contained in limitations
Allowing campfires during migrations!

This fire could have pluses and minuses!
Fire wars have become very dangerous
Dynamite, Nuclear Bombs and Missiles!
Many discoveries have multiple uses,
Requiring both social ethics and morals!

While daytime has economics concerns!
Night time continues to us to entertain!
Now electrical lights produced by energy
Provides us waking time pleasantries!
Providing rhythms for work and leisure!

Care illustrates our human creativity.
Inspiring further advanced discovery!
We have inherited these advancements
Thereby learning human enhancements!
Blessed by ages of human inheritance!

AN ATTITUDE of GRATITUDE

By practicing more personal gratitude
We express a more positive attitude!
This provides numerous advances!
Shown by both faith and sciences!

Thankfulness strengthens resistance!
This attitude bolsters immune systems!
It can also lower human blood pressure!
Contributing to our experience of pleasure!

Gratitude also helps better sleeping!
Likewise multiplies by healthier eating!
Then we feel more refreshed awakening!
Plus, benefits greater interest in exercising!

We recover from trauma more quickly!
Gratitude reduces depression and anxiety!
Thereby providing us greater happiness!
We experience less isolation and loneliness!

When we express "Thank You" graciously!
A sensitive receiver smiles appreciatively!
Through practicing "How can I help you?"
Can also enhance our own competence!

Rather than stating refusals as "I can't"
Is conveyed more positively as "I don't."
You can state "No" and not feel guilty,
Provides honest response very readily!

"Let's go!" leads onward to adventure!
With appreciative eagerness for sure!
Practicing "Yoga" can be invigorating!
Along with our personal meditating!

Gratitude helps us to be faithful!
Thankful and faithful as we fulfill!
Expressing thanks to our Creator!
Helps us to even become healthier!

What faith has long already known[7]
Sciences[8] confirm by data shown!
Confirmation displays compatibility
Inspiring us to live more thankfully!

---

[7] Psalm 100, Luke 22: 17-18, Acts 24: 3 in Bible.
[8] Research by University of California, Berkeley scientists! Dallas Morning News, 12/31/2014

ASSERTIVE POWER!

Power is an elusive human expression!
　Expressed excessively or with discretion!
　　How do human use power appropriately!
　　　So that this power is expressed ethically?

History reveals the fitting and abusive!
　Difficult to assess as human motives!
　　Controls may be present or absent!
　　　In order to set appropriate limits!

Human reactions are unpredictable!
　Under pressure and threat inexplicable!
　　Most persons recognize this problem!
　　　In addressing what to recommend!

This literary piece has hesitation
　The writer gives varied recognition!
　　With trepidation and hopefulness
　　　Let us proceed with carefulness!

AGGRESSIVE USE of POWER

Unconscious use and abuse or power
　Contrasting with conscious users!
　　Often aggression can be spontaneous
　　　Used without balancing impulsiveness!

Power by humans is ambiguous!
　Used unconsciously and conscious!
　　Power may be open or disguised!
　　　Often power is used by surprise!

Authority figures express power!
Parents control those younger!
Teachers use class discipline!
Police control criminal and victim!

Adults may be abusive to children!
Spouses may control their mates!
Police can arrest the suspicious!
Robbers may become malicious!

RECOGNIZING AGGRESSION

Bullying can be done openly
Picking victims quite instantly!
Some victims prompt bullying!
Bully-victim make a "pairing!"

Bosses have major responsibilities!
Then subordinates become utilities!
Government leaders have authority!
Governing people in their citizenry!

Assumptions see power consciously!
Abuses may be done unconsciously!
Neither party may have awareness!
Until abuses become obvious messes!

Professionals may overwhelm clients!
Physicians may over-control patients!
Clergy may serve as if they are God!
Judges may make their rulings weird!

C. EXPLORING

Explorations are what people do;
We like to find something new!
This is an exciting process;
It takes energy and rest.

We do discover new finding!
The Universe is always waiting.
Technology helps these processes;
These actions are scientific tests!

We build upon previous discoveries;
Trying to solve previous mysteries.
These are recorded in "histories;"
Now part of ancient stories.

C. LEGAL ISSUES:

WHAT ARE ABUSES of POWER?

Is capital punishment abusive?
Debate now continues as useful!
What is bases for death sentences?
Can humans decide without biases?

Do humans have rights for guns?
Is it provided in 2nd amendment?
To bear arms as a personal right?
Only intended for national defense?

How can Presidents legally initiate war?
Or does Congress serve as the "Decider?"
After WW II, has this been abused?
Consider how this power is used!

Korean War had no Congressional approval!
Over 50,000 American casualties resulted!
Plus, Vietnam was the "American War!"
Bay of Tonkin Resolutions undeclared!

Are these abuses or are they neglect?
Is combat against ISIS ever correct?
Obama sought Congressional approval!
To declare war limited to three years!

Ambiguity continues for starting wars!
When invasions do occur, it is clearer!
Attacks by any terrorists is a puzzle!
No nation is considered as terrorists!

WHAT IS OUR DUTY?

Soldiers report to duty in uniform!
U.S. is defended by men and women!
Soldiers will obey as their orders!
Defending U.S. interests and borders!

Volunteers have not been enough!
Without a draft, this is very tough!
"Private contractors" do our bidding!
Private authority, not military drilling!

But contracting has become abusive!
Haliburton and subsidiaries included!
Contractors outside of military authority!
Confusing discipline and responsibility!

V-P Cheney was CEO of Haliburton!
Insiders 2001-9, this was uncertain!
Private contractors are "only for profit!"
This arrangement does not deserve credit!

PRE-EMPTION

Pre-emptive ideas of war are dubious!
Bush/Cheney Administration used this!
The Iraq War has become a real disaster!
Over 5000 Americans casualties suffered!

Innumerable Iraqis injured or dead!
Numerous veterans became injured!
Brain injuries, loss of limbs, PTSD!
These problems are carried home!

By 2014, estimate $1.7 trillion expended!
Cost of victims' care is not even included!
Economists estimate $3 trillion overall
What can justify this pre-emptive war?

Pre-emption is seen as not being attacked!
But speculation pre-emptors might act!
Pre-emptors take initiative before attack!
What justifies preliminary war action?

MORE AMBIGUITY

Reagan, 1983, had Congressional approval,
But actual war in Lebanon did not occur
His invasion of Grenada not acted upon!
1991 attack on Iraq for occupying Kuwait!

No Congressional declaration in 1991
To invade and occupy Afghanistan!
In 2003, Bush/Cheney beyond Congress
Invaded Iraq so two wars were pursued!

GOVERNMENTS

Political leaders can abuse authority!
Unaware they can act unconsciously!
Presidents, Royalties and Dictators
May not recognize they are abusers!

America's three branches of government!
Serving to balance power of their offices!
Examples of abuse are very numerous!
Pretending as civil servants is dubious!

Congress may control or neglect!
Legislative proposals as their acts!
Supreme Court may act like God!
Presidents may wield power as a rod!

Governments may engage in war!
Identifying enemies to slaughter!
These aggressive actions can occur!
To overwhelm enemies as others!

WEALTH

Superiority deceives many wealthy
That they should dominate lowly!
Unequal power is exerted frequently!
By leading poor persons into slavery!

Control is assumed by the wealthy!
Tempting them to dominate cruelly!
Justice often favors the controllers
Stifling the lives of those poorer!

Money is abused by many in power!
Rather than a resource as sharers!
Passing on the wealth to inheritors
Perpetuates inequities to successors!

Assumption of power is contagious!
Frequently this is very unconscious!
This can result in serious injustice!
Social problems can become a mess!

PASSIVE USE of POWER

Ignoring problems becomes passive!
Not recognizing what are injustices!
When citizens do not become active
Persons may not know how to live!

Passive aggression is very slippery!
But adolescents learn this quickly!
Agree with the authority figures;
Then do not comply as actors!

People who utilize nonviolence
Misunderstood as being passive!
But nonviolence can be very active!
Defeating those who are aggressive!

When controlled by aggression
Different tactics for one's actions!
Direct opposition is not warranted
While discipline is recommended!

APPROPRIATE USE of POWER

This topic is very challenging!
How not to become controlling!
Fighting back is not recommended
It results in more violence un-ended!

Violence results in more violence!
A vicious cycle has continuance!
How can humans live peacefully?
By living together respectfully!

Between aggression and passivity
Is "ASSERTIVENESS as priority!
Asserting our own personal rights
Without violating others' rights!

Assertiveness requires discipline,
Controlling one's own reactions
This undoes aggressive actions
By not responding with aggression!

PRACTICES

Instead of accusing other persons
Who often state: "You" accusations!
Reply with one's own responses
"I..." rather than accusatory "You...."

Being in touch with oneself
Helps self-control as ourselves!
Attacking aggressors is unworkable!
This soon heightened confrontations!

Assertiveness stands for one's rights!
Undoing the aggressor's own attacks!
After practice, these are effective
Appropriate and also expressive!

Countering aggression is recommended
Plus, passive-aggression as practiced!
Assertiveness needs personal discipline
To become effective and responsive!

MODERN MENTORING

Mentoring is an important quality!
    By assisting to increase credibility!
Young persons are beneficiaries!
    Mentors are rewarded intangibly!

New value can become strategies!
    For your consideration as qualities!
Add positive! "Encourage-mentors!"
    Mentees gain wisdom of benefactors!

Even further: "Beyonder Mentors!"
    Help mentees go beyond predictors!
By surprising familiar observers
    Assisting those who are similar!

"Encourage-mentors" as positive!
    Countering predictions as negative!
Affirming younger is supportive
    Encourage-mentors are affirmative!

DISCERNING

Discernment is a key capability!
    Discerning truth of possibilities!
By evaluating among alternatives
    In decision processes as positive!

Discern+mentor=Discern mentors!
    Personally, plus internationally!
Weighing options as recommended;
    Valuable in family and community!

Life confronts mentees with decisions!
Deciding what to choose by evaluations!
All of our decisions are significant
Discerners can become important!

CREATING

Balancing conformity and creativity!
Creativeness is a valuable quality!
This step opens "Creative-mentors!"
Encouragement to become originators!

Envisioning possibilities is essential!
For creators to reach their potential!
Favorable envisioning is supportive!
Helping teams to become collaborative!

Discovering new solutions is needed!
Cultures encourage what is expected!
Mentors typically value imaginations!
So, mentors produce original creations!

RISK-TAKING

New products demand risk-taking!
Encouragement to develop undertakings!
Risks flourishes on leading edges!
Exploring builds new knowledges!

The ability to learn from mistakes,
Because fewer mistakes facilitate!
Making mistakes fast is helpful
Learning what needs correction!

Mentoring benefits give many skills!
Ready to engage in change in schools!
Personal sensitivity of key differences
Raises constructive questions and answers!

When to motivate or to wait!
Productive inquiries for bait!
Learn together by collaboration!
Tailoring key future consultations!

Letting go as the younger proceed,
Consult later as there are needs!
For more independent adventures!
Launching themselves to futures!

D. PROCEDURES:

CELEBRATION of MEANING

Why is personal meaning so attractive?
    Is this an experience especially positive?
To curious persons meaning is essential
    To pursue their own lifetime potential!

People with purpose often do thrive,
    Wanting to reach out while they are live!
Meaningful purpose does empower
    Helping one's life to climb up higher!

Meaning does enhance our living!
    So that "receiving becomes giving!"
Investing oneself to be worthwhile
    To let loving others becomes a style!

Meaning is also very inspiring!
    Lifting up one's purpose for living!
Life then becomes more hopeful,
    Eventually becoming consequential!

BY-PRODUCTS

A by-product expresses true happiness!
    Even when experiencing restlessness!
Energy becomes definitely uplifting
    As happiness truly enhances meaning!

Hope draws us to get out ahead!
    It lifts us to rise up to get out of bed!

Our days become full of expectation!
Makes personal meaning a celebration!

Meaning is intangibly an inspiration!
Meaning may not be a direct target!
Meaning often arises as a by-product!
It can draw us forward to go onward!

Likewise, we rarely would be cold
By making a birthday to be our goal!
Rather birthdays are celebrated!
Happening to help us feel elated!

Dreaming adds even more to memories!
Day-dreaming plus our night reveries!
Dreams just happen to be uncontrolled
May compel us to become even bold!

SIGNIFICANCE!

Significance can be mesmerizing!
This should not at all be surprising!
Inspiring us with a reason for being!
Plus enriching us personally for living!

Hoping is clearly very beneficial!
Hope draws us ahead to potentials!
Love that is hopeful is so inherent!
Drawing us upon our deepest roots!

As we search for personal meaning
Life likewise becomes fascinating!
Looking forward is very enhancing
Providing energy for worthy living!

Our meaning calls for celebrating!
It is contagious for others waiting!
Inspirations arise to go on further
Drawing us on our path forward!

CONUNDRUMS

Life complexities are apparent
Reflections have puzzlements!
Baffling even the keenest minds
Curious about what to we find!

Some are simple conundrums!
Others become more profound!
Persons dislike uncertainties!
Puzzled by creation mysteries!

There are convoluted issues;
Others may be trouble-free!
Then there are provocations
Involving many interactions!

Here is one for our consideration:
What is the "Meaning of Creation?"
In contrast to "Creation of Meaning?"
These questions for our considering!

MENTAL WRESTLING

People wrestle with puzzles
Desiring to solve their troubles!
Others may ignore these questions,
Not wanting to have indigestions!

These items may contradict!
Presenting many with conflict!
There are both simple answers
Plus "complicated complexities!"

The meaning of creation
Has countless explanations!
Biology sees advancing genes
Examining all of the means!

Is life perpetuating evolution?
Selectively making contributions?
This calls for more reproduction
Adding to further complexification!

SCIENTIFIC DISCOVERIES

Physics uncovered basic elements!
Billions of years of replacements!
Bacteria eventually did emerge
Into evolving life on this earth!

"The Earth is a Goldilocks planet!"
That is not to Cold and not too Hot!
Water has also been very essential!
For elements to become creatures!

With this expansive universe
Other planets may also converse!
Providing many more questions!
"What is the purpose of Creation?"

Science is basically analytical!
Discovering causal relationships!
This uncovers the ways and means!
Without addressing "Why?" and "Where?"

COOPERATION and COMPETITION

In human experiences, paradox emerges,
    These polarities inherently have truth on both sides.
        These complicated conflicts can contradict or be conflicts.

Where might we search to then be found?
    People have complex natures to swivel around,
        Capacities to destroy simultaneously also abound!

Another duality is feminine and masculine!
    Both are essential as complementary and conflictual!
        Created as separate but also essential for our survival!

Throughout human history tension exists,
    To compete with each other or to be cooperative!
        When one dominates, the contra style can debilitate!

Within families are competition and cooperation!
    Functioning for mutual benefit and also for stimulation!
        Children play together and compete for more attention!

In societies that are productive, tensions exist!
    Pure competition theoretically occurs under conditions!
        When producers create but then do not control distribution!

Agriculture exemplifies pure competition:[9]
    Millions of farmers produce food products readily!
        But they have almost no control of prices for productivity!

---

[9] The Author has been a farmer.

Since their products are perishable in time,
    Farmers are constrained as they all compete!
        But paradoxically, farm families are ready to cooperate!

Fishing industries likewise compete for price!
    Their catches are unpredictable and so are markets!
        Because fish soon perish, they compete for good returns!

Monopolies strive for controlling markets!
    If one produce dominates the field, others suffer!
        Monopolists can control both production & distribution!

Large corporations try to exclude competition!
    By dominating the economics to avoid cooperation!
        Great returns for wealth can result for such a corporation!

On the other hand, workers are vulnerable!
    With many laborers, employers can take control!
        Hiring and wages are not handled by employees but employers!

Consequently, laborers are clearly vulnerable!
    Their wellbeing is primarily control by businesses!
        Workers compete while employers can readily dominate!

These tensions result in differentials in power!
    Unless workers join unions to be jointly together!
        Bargaining equality results in fairer contracts & wages!

Bon-a-fide contracts require equal power,
  Then parties involved can be equal bargainers!
    When inequalities exist, someone will likely suffer!

A clear example exists in medical care!
  Doctors are inordinate power over patients!
    Sick persons are hardly in a position to negotiate!

Both hospitals and professionals dominate!
  Patients have little awareness of eventual costs!
    "Fee-for-service" encourages providers for treatments!

Consequently, medical economics is unfair!
  Fair contracts do not exist now for medical care!
    Medicine tends to be a monopoly rather than fair!

Costs in America are skyrocketing!
  Other advanced societies have less spending.
    Other cultures have even better outcomes occurring!

BANKS and FINANCIAL CORPORATIONS

Providers have advantages like in health care!
  Financial oligarchies have dominating influence!
    Top-down domination result in unfair bargaining!

A Great Recession started in 2007!
  Wall Street Banks and Financiers were competing.
    But clients were vulnerable to the financiers dominating!

Consequently, competition was limited!
  Monopolistic control was a trend in economics!
    Customers became trapped in unethical manipulations!

While a façade of cooperation demised,
  Millions of peoples on the bottom were victimized!
    The economy nearly collapsed due to unfair practices!

While controllers advocate free markets,
  They discover ways to gain unfair advantages!
    When Banks and Financiers failed, they wanted rescues!

When producers dominate, clients are vulnerable,
  Controlling corporations want economics both ways!
    Free markets for them, rescued if they create failures!

Cooperation is rarely dominant currently,
  Competition when it works to for distributions!
    But monopolistic control can dominate in competition.

These tensions occur in paradoxical truths!
  Both cooperation and competition have their place!
    Ethical balance in economics and politics is the essence!

In international trade, inequalities exist!
  Powerful economies can dominate the markets!
    If top-down prevails, the bottoms-up likewise suffers!

Controllers naturally want to dominate!
  Their subjects are vulnerable to such plutocrats!
    Equality is a myth that is rarely experienced to cooperate!

Winner takes all is a zero-sum game!
Such competition is destructive for humanity!
Enlarging the outcomes for all is seen to be ideally!

The paradox of competition<>cooperation
Needs both equitable rules and also regulations.
Humanity can better thrive for ethical formulations!

Pure competition can stymie cooperation.
Complete cooperation stymies competition!
Need balance for optimal human experiences!

E. PHYSIOLOGICAL FACTORS:

What does our brain need to be healthy?
 Yes, our brain needs oxygen and activity,
  Plus, nourishing food for productivity!
 Are these enough for an optimal body?
No, there are other items for creativity!

Naturally, repeating "OHM" after yoga![10]
 It helps our brain and body to be healthy!
  And meditation helps our own vitality!
 Day Dreaming when possible does assists!
Plus, Sleep and Night Dreaming do help![11]

Music contributes to stimulate our brain!
 Plus playing an instrument is a claim!
  Creative activities without a strain!
 Singing aids a brain to deal with pain!
Redirecting our minds to another aim!

In addition, meditation promotes empathy!
 By enhancing our feelings of sympathy!
  Meditation helps our working memory!
 Thereby reducing emotional reactivity!
Yoga allows us to participate playfully!

A facet of yoga redirects our thoughts!
 Opening brain and body to let go of "oughts!"
  We can focus more on original concepts!
 Solving problems that still trouble us!
Discovering effective new approaches!

One of my old students asked an expert:
 Before a test, does a stiff drink help?

---

[10] Bond, Michael, Oct. 2014, "Everybody Say OMM!" <u>New Scientist.</u>
[11] Nuwer, Rachel, Oct, 2014, "The Next 1000 Years," <u>New Scientist.</u>

This authority replied with wisdom!
"Yes, but it is only half a can of beer!"
Relaxing the body from mind from fear!

These items combine to reduce anxiety!
So that one can perform more optimally!
Of course, engage in activities morally!
Otherwise, one might be feeling guilty!
Plus share your best ideas voluntarily!

Creativity is essential to solve problems!
My own doctoral mentor brief definition:
Creativity: "Constructive response to stress!"
Clearly yoga and meditation among the best!
Repeating "OOOOHHHHMMMM" does the rest!

Thanks to David, our excellent teacher!
We have opportunities led by this leader!
My personal experience is now 20 years
Persistent practice becomes contagious!
I recommend we have fun and be curious!

Neuroscience Complexities

With hundreds of billion neurons plus hi-speed connections,
The human brains are "multi-verses" mysterious in creation!
Commonly described as a few pounds of gray raw material,
These internal "universes" intrigue neuroscientist's populations.

Over a century ago, Brocca recognized regions of brain functions,
Contours of skulls were considered to have localized operations.
Recently, Magnetic Radiation Imaging traces blood movement,
More specific regions of a brain are examined for activations.

Explorations of cognitive functioning is complex to localize,

Our Sympathetic Nervous System identifies and synthesizes.
Our amygdala in our primitive brain is activated for protection,
Reflexes are automatically faster than our conscious reaction.

Our Para-Sympathetic Nervous System helps to restore balance,
We cool down to think consciously for our learning experiences!
Fortunately, excitement of our primitive fears prompts survival,
If we are cross-examined, our conscious thoughts are on trial!

Managing our animal instincts with our cognitive intelligence,
Are major challenges to build our skills physically and mentally.
As human beings, we have capacities for creative development,
Our potential contributions are the challenges for humanity!

For very personal lab learning, I demonstrated our reactions!
I would come into the room very seriously and deliberately!
With a stern demeanor, I would state: "Put away your books,"
"I am giving a pop quiz!" after grading their first examination.

"Take out a clean sheet of paper and number one, two, three!"
Thereupon, I would take chalk to begin writing down a question!
After finishing the first one, I would start writing the second one,
The nervous tension in complete silence was now very palpable,

With 30-40 seconds of stern tension, I would turn with a smile,
"We're not having a pop quiz! This is a lesson on nervous system!"
Faces registers relief! Smiling laughs spontaneously appeared,
Once I actually heard a faint "You Son-of-a-Bitch" was uttered!

Immediately, I asked the class to express how they initially felt:
Responses included: I breathed heavily," "Stomach discomfort!"
"I started to sweat!" "I sunk down in my chair!" "I worried!"
"This is your experiential lectures 'Sympathetic Nervous System!'"

Every student is encouraged to jot down these and others feelings!
Their amydala reacted with alarm, fear, hatred and feeling fearful!

After two minutes to remember their negative emotional reactions,
   By this time, almost everyone was smiling, taking big "breath full."

Quickly, I would pose: "What were your own immediate reactions
   When I turned around, smiled to say, 'This is not pop quiz today!'
Hilarious comments flooded the room with of emotional relief,
   "Jot these down because this is your lecture registered in emotions!"

Their initial fearful reactions are "The Sympathetic Nervous System."
   They could read the current chapter for even more systematic details!
When safety was assured, their Para-Sympathetic Nervous System,
   Many told me that, they never forgot that laboratory experience!

To capture a visual image, I lifted a map that revealed Garfield!
   Dressed in academic regalia and with a non-typical stern look!
His caption says: "I have a Pop Quiz, and I not scared to use it!"
   This comic express is perfect to "debrief troops in their combat!"

Visual and Auditory Class Demonstrations

People are very interested in understanding their own behaviors,
   Laboratory and contrived class experiences are so invaluable.
When learners personally experience key concepts for learning,
   Their lasting experiences are unequalled for their experiencing.

I have classroom experiments that liven up lectures and readings,
   Several deal with the special "teamwork" of our human senses,
Both visual depth perception and auditory localizing are unique,
   Timely questions for explanations stimulate further inquiries.

One visual experience requires each subject to have dark glasses.
    With the viewers facing perpendicular to a swinging pendulum
And one eyes covered by dark glasses, optical illusions may be seen.
    The pendulum does not appear to swing in just one visual plane.

The pendulum appears to subjects with depth perceptual differences.
    It appears to swinging in an elliptical circle but not back and forth.
Then when I place part of my body in front of the peak of the swing,
    The pendulum strangely appears to be going right through my
    body!

The auditory localization class lab is too complicated to describe,
    Again, students learn the advantages of having two ears for
    hearing.
Sensing the direction of the source of a sound is a social behavior.
    In dangerous environments, locating a sound is critical for
    survival!

Descriptions verbally are not a substitute for experiential learning,
    So, the following is only an introduction needing more elaborating.
The Teamwork of Senses is readily demonstrated outside or in class,
    Forming teams of four, is a safe turf to consider even more ideal!

Balance, Vision, Hearing Teamwork

Spacing teams out for room with these guides: "Ask for a volunteer!"
    "Who has typical balance, sight and hearing! Others in a circle!"
Ask the volunteer subject: "Stand on one foot and tell what you feel!"
    Most can balance on one foot while catching oneself it can happen.

"Discuss what the volunteer states about their standing on one foot."
    Then "Instruct the subject to shut their eyes and stand on one
    foot!"
"Catch them is they start falling!" "Discuss what the subject reports!"
    "What sensations in the ankles, legs and upper body that do recur."

Third trial: "Spin around three times rapidly and stand on one foot!"
"Team members be near, alert to catch if subject starts falling down!"
"Ask volunteer subject to describe bodily sensations and thinking!"
Very few subjects are able to spin and stand up with their eyes shut!

Prompt the whole class to explain how sensory experiences are working.
"What type of teamwork is occurring in these successive experiencing?"
After time deliberation, identify how the balance of our vestibular,
The sight of visual horizon, and the kinesthetic sense is functioning.

Benefits from experiential learning a memorable for learners to know,
Demonstrations may prompt learners to study key chapters further.
Moreover, the variation of in-class experiments demonstrate research,
Team discussions add to individual insights that help beneficially.

Multi-Taskers or Modern Con-Artists?

"Hi-Techies" in this gadget generation are known also as "Tech Savants!"
With the latest "electronic communication device" they work like ants!
Techies do not run on four legs like ants but go with hi-tech equipment,
They have very agile thumbs but the rest of their body suffers neglect!

We will return to the ant metaphor when this piece is brought to a close,
First, it is essential to evaluate the comparisons of hi-tech multi-taskers!

Among the younger generations, there are phenomenal communications,
> Parties can link with persons around the world to gain more preparation!

These devices for communicating have mushroomed recently and rapidly,
> Far beyond the capacities of past generations considered condescendingly.

Facebook and Twitter have abbreviated internet and e-mail communications,
> Almost instantaneous connections permit brief messages in these relations.

Multi-taskers claim proficiency in electronic messaging and photo messaging,
> Their array of equipment and programs is impressive but also misleading!

They assume that all the different tasks they do are of superior qualities,
> In these quests for the latest messaging, they are subject to vulnerabilities!

Five Potential Vulnerabilities

Now these criticisms may unlikely be immediately recognized by hi-techies,
> So, denial is a likely defense they will express as part of their own styles.

You are advised to take each with a grain of salt for future consideration,
> When postulated research delivered even more evidence for deliberation!

1st obvious criticism to recent "Tech Savants" is this evidence is premature!

Each one of these five discoveries is deniable by participants in this venture.

Multi-taskers are often convinced that they can process multiple activities,

The rush of both messages and communications equipment faces realties.

First, the criticism recent tech savants are blind to technology etiquette!

They are constantly fussing with their favorite equipment often in public.

Whatever they possess starts to possess their attention and involvement,

Savants will interrupt most social gatherings with messages as precedence.

Checking e-mail messages goes constantly as if they are the center of attention,

Face-to-face companions are cut off when a message comes to awareness!

Web surfing is constantly attracting them to neglect of immediate persons,

During lectures, sermons and class activities, they are involved in distractions.

These "hi-tech addicts" fail to recognize that persons are talking with them,

Their addiction is so ingrained that they may be failing in social courtesies!

Quick apologies can leave others skeptical in these narcissistic narrow realms,

No longer naturally gravitating toward courtesy they become Tech Savants!

Secondly, hi techies may not actually realize they are hurting their brains!

If requested to forego browsing the internet, iTunes of anything else again.

In just a few minutes, conditioned brains want this kind of instant stimulation,

They may claim to be multi-focused claiming to want a prodigy recognition.

Evidence is showing that multi-taskers perform worse than non-multi-taskers

On many categories including critical thinking skills and also memory tests.

Understandably, they have difficulties in noticing the other persons' emotions,

They have less gray matter in their brains, but may deny these realizations.[12]

Thirdly, techies are showing tendencies to dislike conversing face-to-face!

They are caught up in their equipment they fail to talk with one another!

The tech equipment has actually provided ways to avoid talking with others,

They do not regularly engage in long conversations with sisters or brothers.

We do enjoy our interactions with acquaintances without having a contract

They can take their equipment into a restroom and continue to be in contact!

When engaging such Tech Savants, the engagement will be dependably brief,

You will not need to go the bathroom first in order to preclude needing relief!

---

[12] Lamberti, P., February, 2012, "Tech Savants," The Rotarian.

Fourthly, another major finding if their only news comes from Facebook!

> With such limited time for lengthy reports, they rely on biased quicky blurts!

A study found an average undergraduate today spends two hours on Facebook!

> By not watching nightly news, they primarily rely on friends to give quotes!

The immediate problem is that most Facebook partners are ill informed, too,

> Many hi-techies cannot be considered reliable on conveying critical news!

Techies falsely have the impressions that they are in touch with the world,

> But confirming evidence shows that their global scope has been narrowed!

Fifthly, there is increasing evidence how our technology affects emotions,

> Without having constant hi-tech linkage, they become depressed and anxious!

When are expected to give up networking, emailing, Web-surfing and texting,

> Descriptive outcomes are evidence of addiction, depression and withdrawing.

Moreover, consistent with previous items, they find themselves feeling lonely,

> They find even conversing on a telephone would be "too weird" reportedly.

They may feel that their cell phones had become an extension of themselves,

> Many become personally vulnerable to overwhelming emotions of grieving.

When students take breaks of 48-hours, they will focus on persons around,

> Some conclude that they are vulnerable to the downsides of multi-tasking.

There is a recovery of realizing that they will not let technology rule them,

> Rather, by taking precautions to preclude addiction, they will be in control!

So What?

So what do you conclude?-Is "hi-teching" now here to stay or will it go away?

> Self-evaluating can be done with fuller awareness of implications that stay!

Our brains function without hi-tech electronics that can never replace it,

> Can we supplement appreciation while taking precautions as we notice?

The five reasons mentioned above are options to notice, not fixed in concrete!

> There will be more electronic devices that will be replete and will fascinate!

As long as we use our freedom to choose, our brains will still maintain control,

> When machines and technology are attractive, we should let them take over!

F. CULTIVATING our HUMAN GIFTS:

Our human bodies are amazingly complex
        From bones and muscles for standing erect!
Plus, seven senses working as a team!
        Plus, our brains are miraculously keen!

Animals also compose our gifts!
        As living creatures of this earth!
Humans Beings are interdependent
        Each with a mind for us to think!

Thoughts are complicated qualities
        First, concrete about many tangibles!
As a brain grows, comes abstractions
        To think of thoughts like perceptions!

A brain with 100 billion neurons
        Plus, trillions of connecting axons!
This brain is between our ears!
        Combining thoughts we can share!

SPECIAL SIGNIFICANCE!

Humans are the epitome of Creation!
        Creativity, intelligence, imagination!
For ideals, evils, relations and realism;
        Inventions, romance, poetry, theorems!

We can also create nasty conflicts!
        Including anger, wars and arguments!
Gifts to solve problems peacefully
        Correct violence, poverty and inequalities!

Growth of our brains is essential,
        To master Earth's environmental!

But our own invasive propensities
  Along with new projectile missiles!

Surprisingly violence is reducing![13]
  From 10,000 years of researching!
Humans are lessening hostilities
  Resolving some problems peacefully!

SOLVING PROBLEMS,
Not MAKING THEM!

Current challenges are now global!
  Climates growing! Pollution horrible!
Our actions need to be responsible!
  Protecting life and planet world-wide!

There is need for "hyper-pro-sociality!"[14]
  Including cooperation and collaboration!
Over-ruling territoriality to master
  So, humans do not make disasters!

With over seven billion now on earth
  We hope to help showing our worth!
Trillions of ants work cooperatively![15]
  But can humans also act positively?

As human beings, we can learn!
  To protect our own environment!
Reducing fossil fuels making CO2
  To preserve both earth and lives!

---

[13] Pinkston

[14] Morean, C.R., August 2015, "The Most Invasive Species of All," Scientific American.

[15] Wilson, E.O. Extensive research on Ants Globally.

CONFLICT MANAGEMENT!

Self-interests can become rampant!
　　Unless addressed with alternatives!
Hostilities also need to be managed
　　So weak are protected by advantaged!

Artificial barriers must come down!
　　Racism, exploitations, angry frowns!
National boundaries made by man,
　　Separate humans on related-lands!

"Compartmentalizations" are artificial!
　　Plus, unfair and biased criminal trials!
Corrections need to be fairer!
　　When justice is administered!

Economic distribution of wealth,
　　Hopefully improves human health!
Political systems be representative!
　　For decisions of social legislation!

COMMUNITY

Species develop their communities!
　　Supporting and controlling offspring!
Socializing is a common experience,
　　Protecting their own for existence!

Rare creatures are self-reproducing;
　　Most have patterns for courting and mating!
Perpetuating their young for generating!
　　Teaching them processes for surviving!

Species may devour theirs for food!
　　Nature is interdependent to do good!
Many species threatened with extinction
　　Humans have responsibilities for protection!

Accountability requires careful monitoring!
　　Human ingenuity finds this very demanding!
Protecting our environments is a challenge!
　　For "Husbanding" this very fragile planet!

RECOVERING OUR PURPOSE

Does life on earth have a purpose?
　　Or is life an accident on this earth?
Evolving by chemical elements joining
　　Without a destiny to be pursuing?

With purpose, we have more worth!
　　To discover our "nitch" from our birth!
Perhaps to explore and enjoy creation
　　Using our creativity and imagination!

To seek and to research wonders?
　　So that we may become appreciators?
The Universe is very miraculous!
　　Our minds are conscious and unconscious!

Unconsciousness comes to awareness,
　　Contributing to knowledge established!
Expanding our insights of unknowns;withw
　　We recognize what become knowns!

FATHOMING

We discover major gift of humanity!
    Using our senses and brains scientifically!
Intangible thoughts become tangible!
    Abstract ideas transform to be concrete!

Searching become our challenges!
    Stretching our minds to find purposes!
Knowledge thereby expands rapidly
    Human beings utilize technologies!

A 1000 years are possible to imagine!
    Drawing posterity to expand visions!
Heights, Depths, Widths and Breaths
    Plus, more dimension beyond our grasp!

Exploring Human-Divine understanding
    These dimensions for more creating!
We try to fathom our special relating!
    Enriching our lives as God's own Beings!

OLDER ADULTHOOD CONFLICTS: RESOLVING TENSIONS of CRUELTY with EMPATHY

Maturation provides a sanctuary to give attention to conflicts,
    Cruelty of past years confronts Empathy within certain limits.
The heat of passions may be subsided creating some balances,
    These opportunities can afford the luxury of helpful alliances.

The powerful tensions of youth plus young adulthood and later,

May be reduced so parties address conflicts some even better.
Demands of parenting may evolve to the joys _"Grand-parenting."_
Then several generations can optimize equitably joint timing.

Adults in normative health may entertain providing a Legacy,
These are both tangible and equal fully much more intangibly.
"Legacy Builders" can go beyond financial to what is important,
Reflective senior adults can hope to leave something significant.

Monetary legacies assume that the parents have residual wealth,
In contrast, intangible recognitions are so good for one's health.
Symbolic legacies have a different impact depending on what,
This "what" becomes "whys" of "forgiving this and also that!"

These senior years can struggle with productivity and standards,
Ego Integrity holds many wrenching conflicts in for repairs.
The senior may have ambivalence not knowing what to ask,
While simultaneously knowing what more to have as requests.

As adulthood provides sanctuary away from brash struggles,
Mature persons that now no longer live in artificial bubbles;
With the insights of helpers who know the next step passages.
Hearts are responsive discovering positively good messages.

So, _"Legacy Leavers"_ can set a future heritage of real worth,
With a motivation of serving people live right here on Earth.
Dedicated to improving conditions so that people can thrive,
Which is a much better goal that just helping human survive.

G. CROSS-CULTURAL CONTRIBUTIONS

Over decades, cross-cultural experiences,
Contribute to my personal enrichments!
These mostly happened beyond college,
While providing valued experiences!

While I was serving in the Air Force
Stationed near Albuquerque, N. Mexico,
Our Squadron had men from other cultures
Including Blacks and Mexican-Americans.

As Squadron Adjutant with many duties
I learned about soldiers from cultures.
Naturally, we had a number of Hispanics
Who sought this base for assignments.

These were very conscientious personnel,
Very capable of being of being mechanics.
They handled aircraft very conscientiously;
Proud to be serving in the nation's military.

I recall they were very respectful,
Displayed in their job performance.
They earned their military rank
They earned the pilot's thanks!

Mexican food became a treat;
I love enchiladas for a meal to eat.
Food becomes an expression of culture
So today are many Mexican restaurants.

I wish that I had learned to speak Spanish
We need to learn more than only English.
Multiple languages are now essential
Enriching most everyone's potential.

ANCIENT CIVILIZATIONS

Early civilizations struggled for survival!
  The survivors learned from trial and error!
    All benefit from these tough procedures!
  Gradually evolving to pass to youngsters!
As early civilizations emerge to successors!

Yes, women and children were laborers
  Plus, non-dominant males as survivors!
    Together they developed tribal behaviors!
  By archaeology we learn of contributors!
Who were born, lived, worked as providers!

Hunters were key in these migrations
  To follow game as hunter education!
    Many eons were needed with dedication!
  Our ancestors developed by progression;
Descendants learned by selective evolution!

Safety was critical for their survival!
  Leaders gained control of descendants!
    They could demand utmost allegiance!
  So that survivors became descendants!
We are indebted to this type of obedience!

Unfortunately, wars ensued to endure!
  Tribes rarely knew if they were secure!
    Warriors were needed even to suffer!
  Their lives were lost to protect tribes
This provided that members survived!

Ancient rules captured women and children!
  Males were eradicated as an old practice!
    These primitive guidelines are powerful

So that warriors today find them useful!
But future eons need what is functional!

Currently, we know little of predecessors
We are indebted to these as survivors!
We can recognize them as successors!
Our genes and environment are indebted
To these predecessors to be enlightened!

There are several European cultures,
That have influenced my awareness.
Western Europeans countries first
Including Swedish and Norwegian.

With an Economics Professor in 1973,
We engaged students in these cultures.
Our hosts were very conscientious;
These exchanges were precious.

We also visited Denmark and Norway
Plus, Paris, Amsterdam on New Years Day.
They were capable in speaking English
So, we only learned very little Swedish.

My ancestors came from Western Germany
But our own schedule was very inflexible.
But this was followed by other visits
Among them were visits with Swiss.

Zurich is home for the Psychiatrist Jung;
On study leave, two Professional courses.
Then Rome and Vienna were visited
Broadening what I really appreciated.

Other colleagues became good friends.
These are all Western-based cultures.

Subsequent travels were broader;
They were a delight to cover.

These experiences were beneficial,
Interdisciplinary and cross-cultural!
My own teaching was influenced
To do broad education of students.

I began teaching global policy,
As part of our Policy Studies.
One focus was health care;
Also, upon therapeutic care.

As a Texas Licensed Psychologist
For Counseling and as a Therapist;
Plus "Violence and Terrorism;"
Plus, "Dangers of Communism."

Thereupon, came an opportunity
For more on U.S.A. International Policy.
This was a Sabbatical in Washington, D.C.
At the Center for Peace and Public Policy.

My Wife and Son accompanied me.
We all responded very positively.
We did both conferring and learning,
Plus, cultural events that were happening.

Moreover, there are historical sites,
Recognizing famous Statesmen.
Plus, the American treasures;
Visitation at one's leisure.

Two Houses of the U.S. Congress
Plus, famous historical museums.

Musical concerts and visual arts,
And travel assistance in carts.[16]

Washington D.C. is our national Capitol;
Americans are typically very curious.
Both interesting and also serious;
Highly recommended for visitors.

INVITATION to RUSSIA

USA vs. USSR had polarization;
During 1950-1988 was high tension.
Two Superpowers with nuclear weapons;
Powers with greatly tensed apprehension.

Both vying to dominate the world!
Both had their big flags unfurled!
USSR touted their own Communism;
Vying with America in a collision.

Having been an Air Force Nuclear
Officer
I closely watched the tense negotiators.
And having written on "Enemy-Making;"
I hoped for greater nuclear peace-making!

The National Council of Churches,
Made efforts to be arbitrators.
Delegation of Church Leaders
Showing steps to be peacemakers!

These experiences were beneficial;
Interdisciplinary and cross-cultural!

---

[16]   Arlys, my first wife, suffered from crippling arthritis.

My own teaching was influenced,
For broad education of students.

I began teaching Global Policy,
    As part of our Policy Studies.
        One focus was health care;
            Also, upon therapeutic care.

        As a Licensed Psychologist,
    For Counseling as a Therapist.
Plus "Violence and Terrorism,"
And "Dangers of Communism."

Thereupon, came an opportunity;
    For more on international policy.
        A Sabbatical in Washington, D.C.
            "Center for Peace, Policy and Theology!"

        I wrote chapters on national policy;
    Along with a colleague for study.
This recorded these key events,
Usable for future college lectures.

        The National Council of Churches
    Made real efforts to be arbitrators.
A large delegation of Church leaders
Showing steps to build peace-making.

Among the other 250 delegates
    Three of us were from Texas.
        Hosted by Russia's Government
            And the Russian Orthodox Church.

        Our visits were very well planned;
    Twelve teams differently scheduled.

First, we landed in Moscow, the Capitol
Then the teams each had itineraries.

My teams went to Vladimir-Suzdal
Initial Capitol for Prince Validmir.
In 988 A.D., this became his home;
To establish their new Empire.

Our team leader arranged for me,
And the Hosts and Guests exchange.
To dialogue with their own leaders,
And to show we were all appreciators.

We also were hosted in Vladimir,
Named after their first leader.
These were very cordial affairs
Facilitated by times to share.

Then our group went to Estonia,
We landed in their Capitol City
This small nation on Baltic Sea.
Had Scandinavian influences.

We toured a large Collective Farm;
Lead by the Foreman who could charm,
On behalf of our group, I thanked him,
Tying a big red bandana as our gift.

When traveling, I take along bandanas;
Most people recognize them from Texas.
Bandanas are so easy to bring along
Better than speaking far too long!

In Moscow in the Kremlin twice
Once for an opera performance!
A light opera done far too serious
It was "The Barber of Seville!"

After touring sites in Moscow,
We were fed good Russian caviar.
We were hosted by Church Leaders
Including their leading Arch-Bishops.

East of Moscow is an Orthodox Center:
Two Seminaries and large Churches.
We stood for the Worship Services,
Because they do not have pews.

A press conference in the Kremlin:
Four Soviet reporters knew English.
This was an informative occasion,
So, they asked for our observations.

Since my research was on "Enemy-Making"
They found this topic very interesting.
I stood up to make my brief remarks
Immediately they took my photos.

This photo printed in the <u>Moscow News!</u>
Russians knew we were exchanging views.
Later the Russian reporters came to Texas;
We then also had very interesting exchanges.

Upon return to our homes in America
There was wide interest and inquiries.
New media wanted to have reports
Community groups and Churches.

THEN AGONIZING DECISIONS!

Later in 1984, another invitation,
As Team Leader of 25 persons!
1986 would prepare for 1988 trip
To celebrate 1000 years of Christians.

Then I accepted to do planning,
1000 delegates commemorating!
This was preparation in June, 1986.
At the Orthodox Seminary, New York.

First week in New York orientation
Then two weeks as guests of Russians.
For 1000 years in 1988 as Christians,
To know how to deal with questions.

By June, my Wife was weakening;
So, I struggled while deciding.
I resigned as a Leader for 1988.
It was fitting to not further wait.

Her arthritis was progressing;
So, my role was to do caring.
1987, her illness was advancing;
In May, 1988, she was terminating.

Arlys died on May 20th 1988.
Fifty-four years of age that date.
My Daughter, Son and I cried.
We had many decisions ahead.

Two memorial services were held;
The Church she was Ordained Elder!
Second, the "Home Church" in Iowa.
This was also included her burial!

Her basketball teammates all came!
They were Honorary Pall-Bearers.
I was exhausted with grieving,
Reflected in my words speaking.

The grave visited by classmates;
Recalling Old School Classes;
My Sister. Brother plus mates,
Supportive like Daughter and Son.

We had a tombstone erected;
Originally ground of family farm.
Our Faith held us steadfast;
Even when we were downcast!

H. FROM DEFICITS to FULLY OPERATIONAL

Media news often broadcast "deficits!"
    Using this term to describe economics.
        However, a number of deficits now exist!
        Including attention to deficits that persist!
    These persons who cannot keep focused!
They are easily distracted and disturbed!

Attention deficits interfere with learners
    By lacking continuity, challenges teachers!
        Students can be restless while sitting
        Plus bothering classmates by wiggling!
    Some are unable to study a book!
Jumping from pages just to look!

They enjoy pictures, photos and images!
    Plus, the characters who are very visible!
        However, Algebra is still beyond this group
        But, numbers can be possible as concrete!
    They can be happy, sad or disappointed,
With special feeling inside that register!

As abstract thinking at about 12 years
    Concrete thinking is not readily converted!
        Stories need re-teaching after 12-13.
        Abstract ideas now are developing.
    So that theories of ideals really begin!
Coaching and teaching help progression!

Piaget's stages of thinking are helpful
    Outlines how humans develop "knowing!"
        Sequences include concrete operations
        Then followed by formal operations!
    Now operations we will be considering
Building on previous with new thinking!

FORMAL OPERATIONS

"Thinking about thoughts" than follows;
Adolescents can formulate their ideals!
By thinking about future projections!

About what they might and could become!
They may also develop imaginary audience!
Who will watch them in next appearance!

Formulas can be also comprehended
As symbols express new concepts!
Algebra to geometry can be handled!

Also, abstract theory of possibilities!
Scientific ideas can be understood!
Linguistic ideas also appreciated!

When a new theory is first introduced,
Connecting to concrete things can help!
Followed quickly with abstract concepts!

Learning can become accelerated rapidly!
Employing available skills for building
Ideas contrary-to-fact for imagining!

Advanced thinking allows more knowing
In philosophy known as epistemology!
Piaget's stages are epistemological!

Useable in understanding humans!
Critical thinking is very significant!
Creative thinking is its complement!

Focused brains are human talents!

Thinking past, present and futures!
Visionary thinkers are very essential!

For societies to reach for potentials!
Cultivating physical and mental abilities
To optimize collective opportunities!

BEYOND HOMO SAPIENS

Are human brains the ultimate?
Or just prior to the penultimate?
Are there even more that await?

These questions pose us with bait!
So higher intelligence is fascinating!
Life evolves billions of years awaiting!

Can homo sapiens accept even more?
About millions of planets even galore!
Does Our Creator stop just with us?

Infinitesimal among expanding universe!
Can we assume exclusive intelligence?
Would not be a position of arrogance?

Might humans admit as not the epitome?
Recognizing and encouraging real humility!
Christians recognize God is Omniscient!

Omni-present, Almighty, Omni-conscious!
Qualities that prompt worship and admiration!
Aware we are created with finite termination!

We best recognize unknown mysteries!

Many scientists admlt to uncertainties!
What unfolds beyond we can ponder!

Human limitations await for "Beyonders!"
Human creativity, intelligence, imagination!
May be "Beyond" not knowing all Creation!

Future is even beyond that we wonder!
We live in time-space in the present!
Eternity can be imagined in faith!

Beyond unfolds at its very own pace!
Our Where? When? How? and Why?
Probes into our human curiosity!

COMING from BEHIND!
PLASTICITY

Emergence of Resilience

1) If Your team is down 12 points!
Only one quarter left to play!
Will your team make a comeback?

2) Your child is suffering leukemia!
The chances for treatment is 50-60%;
What could you do to make a difference?

3) As husband, Father of two children,
In third military tour in Afghanistan!
How can your whole family respond to his PSTD?

Possible Responses

1) **Your team has come back before!**
> Under pressure, will you win or lose?

Experience making comebacks, chance rise!

2) **Leukemia can be cured:**
> Mother's love expressed early!

Contributes to better resilient prognosis!

3) **Combating "Combat PSTD!"**
> Re-entry adjustment is challenging!

Mutual trust established helps testy time!

Additional Approaches

What helps persons handle these crises?
> Supportive love is essential!

Experience in recovering is critical!

People respond very individually!
> Concerned but not overwhelmed

In-between a wimpy worrier and a toughie!

Surgeons hope patients are fighters!
> Careful listening is vital!

Tolerating manageable pain is essential!

Surgery challenges the whole person!
> But "a fighter" is favorable!

Use less pain medication! Discharged earlier!

Supportive family and faith!
Are plus signs for recovery!
Realistic expectations are plus factors!

Unique Circumstances

Combat veterans have bewildering experiences!
Physical and emotional wounds!
Rehabilitative support with buddies is helpful!

When a veteran is ready to talk confidentially,
Potentially helps down-loading!
Recognition of patriotism by communities!

Recent widowing leaves a grieving gap!
The survivor has lost an anchor!
Support helps healing over time.

Pressurized sports in competition,
These are not life-threatening!
Teamwork and practice plus conditioning assist!!

H. CROSS-CULTURAL CONTRIBUTIONS

I. MULTIPLE APPROACHES

Coming Back Again

Healing is not miraculously instant!
Bouncing back takes patience!
Each person is individually unique!

Resilience is a very favorable quality!
"Resilience Science" has arrived!
Many traditional practices are confirmed!

Special insights are increasing identified:
Mother's love helps from infancy!
Additional pathways to resilience can be applied!

This secure environment fosters trust!
Even when there is much stress!
Trust strengthens persons through life!

In a child's second year, another step:
Caregivers foster a critical factor!
Effective training in "Executive Functions!"

A child learns taking risks to make decisions!
An asset for a lifetime!
Making choices for decisions is a plus!

Norman Garmenzy and Bryon Egeland
Pioneers in resilience theory!
I had graduate courses in Clinical Psychology!

Early favorable environment help,
But most can gain from experience!
Tuning into people's concerns helps resilience!

A key factor is care-giving parents!
Both or at least one is essential!
Effective parents strengthened resilience!

Historical Illustrations

While considering about resilience,
Historical figures illustrate dynamics!
These are brief accounts from media accounts.

Resilient persons from the past century,
Franklin Delano Roosevelt!
He rebounded from polio! Helped develop leadership!

Eleanor Roosevelt symbolizes strength!
Her character inspired the world!
Recovering from the Great Depression and WW II!

"Ike" Eisenhower led Allies and America!
A key General and also President!
He rose to distinction internationally!

Mandela, President of South Africa!
Earlier held 27 years in imprisonment!
He surprised South Africa and all humanity!

World renown, Hillary Clinton!
First Lady, Senator and Secretary of State!
Her strengths involve overcoming setbacks!

Internationally, several did not rebound:
Woodrow Wilson, caved late as President
Richard Nixon finally retreated into ignominy!

Fans were intrigued with Marilyn Monroe!
Drawing attention to her beauty!
Her demise occurred mysteriously by middle years!

IMPRESSIVE RECOLLECTIONS

Persons can see the with hateful violence!
School shootings by angry young males!
They did not sublimate but killed innocent!

Their festering anger burst out of control!
Access to weapons readily discovered!
Killed others violently and also themselves!

Suicidal reactions haunt families and citizens!
Young men wanting attention assert revenge!
Perpetrate horrid killings feeling justified!

From Tragedies to Hopeful Resilience
What are the special dynamics to respond to tragedies?
How can hardy people handle these setbacks positively?

Can persons prepare to constructively address stresses?
Are humans destined to consider life with fatefulness?
We confront struggles with frequent human setbacks!

Attempting to discover strategies when tragedy attacks.
Most heart breaks as very unpredictable surprises,
Catching us unprepared with the onset of these crises.

Is influenced genetically and environmentally!
These interactions motivate activities!
Nature plus nurture involved in interacting!

Cultural Resilience

Individually and culturally combined
"No man is an island to himself!"
Strengths and limitations for best health!

Resilience ultimately cannot conquer all!
Human cultures have their span!
But resilience can optimize realistically!

Does God in the Bible seem to adjust?
Human understanding is anthropomorphic!
Divine-Human interactions are dynamic!

Dynamics possess developmental cycles!
Differentiation in rhythm with integration!
These patterns energize adaptation!

Combined Dynamics

Compelling reasons to be living
Simultaneously "push-and-pull" work together!
Being "drawn and shoved for teamwork!"

Clear evidence may not be accessible!
Reason and Faith are positively interacting!
These are the key verses combing

Multiple variables can be synergetic
Creating jointly greater than expected!
But beware: Some combinations are toxic!

Persistent searching uncovers possibilities!
Resilience science adds more avenues!
When in doubt, then look for clues!

ASSERTING OUR RESILIENCE

HOPE is the keynote of Resilience!
It helps us to cope with persistence!
With illnesses, we also need resistance!
With treatment, we hope for deliverance!

Major religions inspire positive resilience!
Jewish Faith highlights historical deliverance!
Christian Faith prizes continuous faithfulness!
Islam encourages persistent obedience!

Resilience relies on our personal assertiveness!
Overriding both aggressiveness and passiveness!
Our creativity builds hopeful constructiveness!
In order to cope with tempting "negativeness!"

Purposeful living seeks for meaningfulness!
Contributing to our positive creativeness!
Assisting others constructs compliments!
Establishing our experiences in resilience!

NOW and ETERNITY

Now is considered the moment!
Only a quick passing instant!
But an opening to a consultant
About issues that are in ferment!

Ferment suggests a new mixture!
Ingredients blending into a texture!
A recipe for living as ingredients
Creating a product as a resultant!

Products go through a process!
Foods that are tasty to digest!
Metals have strength to resist
Persons with resilience to stress!

We live in a series of moments!
Both short and longer instants!
With experiences that strengthen
To grow resources as a testament!

ETERNITY

Timelessness is unfamiliar to humans!
Our "moments" become a continuum!
Real time is consecutive moments!
Each passing in historical sequences!

Eternity is a very different phenomenon!
It is not like a sequential drama!
All experiences must be right now!
Neither now to then, but all in tow!

Eternity is similar to a photograph!
What you do see and that is all!
There is no movement like a movie!
Everything seems frozen and steady!

While compressed into a moment
Reality is captured in an instant!
Timelessness is all inclusive!
To us humans, it is elusive!

Eternity includes all of our moments!
This is the character of "The Divine!"

God as Trinity is notably sublime!
Eternity is God in Divine Element!

Jesus' Incarnation is God's fleshiest!
Born as a child; grew in adolescence!
Healed, taught as he proclaimed!
Praised, hated, tried and convicted!

Crucified on a cross like a criminal!
Died and Resurrected as Eternal!
Came to us; known as Emmanuel!
Available to all as Lord and Savior!

GERUNDERINGS!

Incarnating, healing, teaching, preaching!
Pleading, forgiving, suffering, petitioning!
Interceding, comforting, feeding, restoring!
Loving, enjoying, holding, embracing!

Resurrecting, appearing, challenging, accepting!
Reincarnating, being, appreciating, recognizing!
Confirming, confronting and complementing!
Ascending, empowering, valuing, leaving!

To be "In Christ" is to be "Eternalizing!"
This state is not actually surprising!
In Christ, With Christ, Through Christ!
Christ is our gift from Divinitizing!

Our God is graciously merciful!
For which we can be very grateful!
Empowered with meaning purposeful!
Included in "The Realm of the Eternal!"

What is Inherent: Evil, Good or "None of the Above?"

What is preventing peaceful cooperation to seek problem solutions?
Why do controversies end in violent hatred with insoluble illusions?
Do human beings suffer from ingrained genes for animosities?
What hampers the human brain from finding nonviolent ways?

Are human just incapable of establishing compatible associations?
What are the deficiencies that result in destructive deformations?
Why is humanity bereft of discovering more constructive outcomes?
When will global nations and individuals discover new remedies?

What factors ignite violence in human frictions and transactions?
Is this destructiveness inherent in our genetic human compositions?
Why does this criminal behavior continue to surface in our existence?
Whatever are these pathologies that persist without our resistance?

These questions are posed to prompt reactions and profound thinking,
In order for people to thrive, these problems need major shrinking!
Humanities' future is still threatened without discovering solutions!
Without new penetrating diagnosis, our efforts are merely illusions!

Probing with More Depth

Deeper fathoming of human beings' problems requires our attention!
Posterity depends upon our deeper deliberate efforts for resolution!
While technical advancements are discovered rapidly with "rapacity,"
Our attention is encouraged for human beings to live more peacefully.

77

Do the old "Laws of the Jungle" still continue in history to prevail?
Or are primitive tribal animosities persisting in our human genes?
What is passed down from past generations is seen as very dubious,
These are precipitating major atrocities experienced by the innocent!

Greek philosophy and mythology provided a good vs. evil dichotomy,
This is also a dualism that simplifies the whole world very conveniently!
The physical is considered evil in contrast to the spiritual seen as good!
The body is evil in contrast with the ethereal mind as it is understood!

This dualism typifies polarizations expressed in dialectical philosophies,
Often leaders contrast the enemy as evil and themselves as heroically.
Throughout much of history, leaders find that enemies are functional,
Providing threats of fear so that power and control become useful!

Too many national leaders want to be a "war leader" seen as heroic!
By announcing a threatening enemy, they strengthen as president!
They acquire more power for claiming to defend their own citizens,
In recent decades, Reagan and Thatcher had enemies contrived!

Margaret Thatcher's leadership was challenged in the early 1980's,
Her power was quickly restored as she declared war on Argentina!
Then Reagan exploited Presidential power as Commander-in-Chief,
His invasion of Grenada in Latin America is parallel in full relief.

Evidence is now accumulating about this extended Bush's Iraq War!
His own leadership was not impressive as "Appointed by the Court!"
His dubious Administration readily developed plans for invasions,
When 9/11 threatened the vulnerability of fears in this nation.

Bush's decisions to invade Afghanistan was launched very ignorantly;
His weak Administration did not comprehend the lessons of
history.
Then his decision to invade Iraq was less informed by intelligence,
Without comprehending the outcomes for the West as a dilettante.

In Depth Analysis

Justin Frank[17] provides helpful windows to fathom Bush and Obama![18]
This psychoanalyst probes from secondary sources for
observations.
These Presidents are not clients so he probes their early development,
He provides very helpful insights in to their functioning as
President!

In both cases he shares in depth interpretations of parents in
childhood,
Plus, the influence of their Grandparents who had significant
input!
He probes the stresses and the gaps that have had far reaching
impact,
Revealing how Bush and Obama learned differently to handle
conflict!

While Bush is driven to be a "Decider" who became impatient waiting,
Obama interior thinking weighs strengths and weaknesses
appearing.
This provides Obama insights into the thinking of other adversaries,
Whereas Bush possessed somewhat less awareness of others'
capacities.

---

[17] Frank, Justin, 2003, <u>Bush on the Couch: Inside the Mind of the President.</u>
[18] _____, 2011, <u>Obama on the Couch: Inside the Mine of the President.</u>

The previous careers of these Presidents also confirm their diversity,
Bush studied at Harvard U. for a Masters in Business Administration.
Obama studied at Harvard in the Law School for an advanced degree.
Bush engaged in business management and Obama in communities.

These contrasts probe questions how government and business compare,
Differential experiences certainly have approaches upon which to bare.
The position of a President has nothing similar with either discipline,
As each President brings both personal and professional experiences.

Bush has a serious limitation in global vision unwilling to save nations,
Instead as a demagogue he wielded American influence for persuasion.
But he lacked the capacities to bring other allies into a strong position,
As he fell into using military power in Iraq and likewise Afghanistan.

Moreover, he and his administration had sparse knowledge of history,
Seemingly unaware of how Great Britain and Russia failed miserably.
Both had invaded Afghanistan in past centuries that resulted in failures,
But the limited knowledge blindsided him in catastrophic decisions.

Frank also makes his observations by inference from their conflicts,
How each manages their aggression learned from early experiences.
Bush typically handles disputes by resorting to simplistic dualism,
Like Reagan, he identifies friends as good while enemies are evil!

Bush tended to surround himself with experts who agreed with him,

Obama seeks wider counsel including parties that disagree with him.

Consequently, he is able to make efforts to practice bipartisan-ship,
Whereas Bush tended to believe others are either for him or against him.

Both of these Presidents according to Frank had "Repetition Obsessions,"
Repeating the behavior and thinking from early childhood experiences.

Obama seeks repeated confirmation so that his decisions are grounded,
Whereas Bush is less reflective so he tends to be more spontaneous!

While erroneous attempts have ascribed these wars to Barack Obama,
More accurately, he inherited wars fought in Iraq and Afghanistan!

<u>Obama's Wars</u>[19] explored his viewpoints about the wars he was handling,
Obama's stance was found in his Nobel Peace Prize speech so revealing!

He reached conclusions very cautiously that "war is sometimes necessary,"
But he then goes on: "war at some level is an expression of human folly!"

Concluding that two Bush/Cheney wars were a major difficult challenge.
The "folly of war" that Obama inherited was derived from revenge!

Justin Frank's recent psychoanalytic books provide external criteria,[20]
This Psychiatrist had built on current contributions to psycho-history.[21]

---

[19] Obama, Barack's acceptance speech for his Nobel Prize for Peace.

[20] Frank, op. cit.

[21] Ibid., 2011, <u>Obama on the Couch: Inside the Mind of the President</u>

This builds on pioneering analyses of Martin Luther and Gandhi,[22]
But not we have contemporary studies of those in the Presidency.

When will leaders learn that destructive wars become devastating?
Now with nuclear weapons, available in arsenals that are waiting!
American intelligence failed about Iraq was very seriously flawed,
While the Bush Administration failed to really have data evaluated!

Enormous costs of human lives and precious resources were utilized,
Civilians are victims while veterans return very damaged or paralyzed!
When will leaders discover a necessity that they should be very cautious?
Because the outcomes about human devastation plus resources wasted!

The distrust of the West that has been engendered in Eastern nations,
It may require many decades of better leadership for global decisions.
Obama was thrust into vaguely defined aggressive actions to fight,
As the decisions by the Bush Administration were far from right.

Encouraging Signs

While the 20th century was notorious for major World Wars I and II,
When millions were killed both soldiers plus civilian including children.
But this past century was not particularly different from prior history,
Because these notorious past wars have incurred numerous casualties.

The encouraging reports are that now we have fewer wars than prior,
Plus, the current wars have fewer deaths, less suffering and orphans!

---

[22] Erikson, Erik, (1993) Gandhi's Search for Truth and (1962) Young Man Luther.

While this may not immediately seem apparently, the data are convincing,
  With discoveries of statistical reports that people may be improving!

Yes, there were atrocities in Bosnia and the Congo plus Mozambique,
  But these have scaled downward with evidence that is very unique!
There may be increasing awareness that wars do not solve problems,
  In fact, wars also cause problems plus resentment leading to revenge!

Since the Viet Nam War, American conflicts have been less destructive,
  The folly of violent wars has been followed by years more constructive.
A few notable developments may have gradually led to improvements,
  These deliberate steps are now worthy because of their significance!

Pope John XXIII distributed an encyclical in 1963 *"Pacem en Terra!"*
  By the 1980's Protestant Churches promoted peacemaking efforts!
In that same decade, America established a "Department of Peace!"
  Balancing previous emphases on Departments of War and Defense.

Conflict management and dispute resolution both came into existence,
  Peacemaking strategies have been effective in negotiating differences.
Progressive measures have also moved onward to "Peace-Keeping!"
  So that in the 21st century attention is given to "Peace-Building!"

Historical research now reveals that fighting wars has begun to wane!
  Shattering centuries of bloody practices, noticeable shift with less pain!
Countries have substantially abandoned war to settle disagreements,
  Even with the Asian and African wars, we now have more settlements!

J. CURRENT RESEARCH FINDINGS

Violence has decreased ranging from spanking children to murders,
   Genocide, tortures and war decreased markedly with more
   nonviolence!
The Better Angels of our Nature: Why Violence has Declined! by
Pinker,[23]
   Sparking a debate whether human nature shifts becoming more
   peaceful.

This author raises questions about how we view our inner motivations,
   Even with the Holocaust, genocidal conflicts and major
   revolutions.
War casualties have plunged very significantly since the mid-1950's!
   More disputes are settled by negotiations even when not apparent!

Pinker also suggests that our better angels include empathy,
self-control,
   Morality and reason have combined to lead to gains in peace
   over war!
Terrorism, murder and other human violence has a downward trend,
   Provoking the issues about whether civilization has taken a new
   bend?

"There really are not many wars anymore!" concludes John Mueller![24]
   These findings are major shifts from former old battles that are
   over.
The Force More Powerful[25] records noteworthy nonviolent successes!
   Resorting to killings hopefully continue to decline as time
   progresses!

---

[23] Pinker, Steven, 2011, The Better Angels of our Nature: Why Violence
Has Declined.
[24] Grier, Peter, December 26, 2011, "Wars grind on; but statistically,
violence declines", The Christian Science Monitor.
[25] Ackerman, P., (editor) et.al., 2000, A Force More Powerful, plus videos
on four continents.

While the current revolutions in North Africa and SW Asia do occur,
　　There has been less bloodshed than traditionally major civil wars!
Whether these lower levels of deaths are due to rapid communication,
　　There are also equivalent claims to recognize improved education!

The side effects of economic globalization are also a major contribution,
　　When vital trading links nations together there are considerations.
Economic ties result in interdependence that has been an extension,
　　So that economic decision-makers have a stake in re-distribution!

Additional encouraging developments are also gradually evolving,
　　There is also a reduction in "structural violence" now unfolding!
Globally, poverty is decreasing during recent decades significantly!
　　The problem needs to be addressed of distributing food equitably!

While the global population may rise from seven to eight billions,
　　The capacity of the planet to produce food is needed for millions.
Scientific improvements are helping, but waste is a major problem,
　　Plus, inequitable global trade agreements under corporate control.

A very noteworthy indicator involves the better education of women,
　　Young girls are increasingly attending schools as well as young men!
When women are educated there are immediate positive outcomes,
　　They become healthier and informed of issues plus fewer children!

Moreover, educated mothers improve the well-being as their families,
　　The children are fed more nutritiously and also healthier hopefully.
Women traditionally have managed explicit aggression more civilly,
　　These developments influence the overt belligerence of men socially.

With current challenges, people are concerned about sustainability!
　　Concern for caring for our environment is pursued more ethically!
The natural resources of the earth, in addition to living organisms,
　　Above all, human life must be highly valued through new prisms!

Beyond concerns for sustainability, health and education of women,
Are the exciting changes in recent decades in forms of government!
Democracy is significantly becoming the governance of more nations,
Autocratic dictatorships are declining that are patriarchal prisons!

Around the world, people are being liberated to experience freedom,
The inherent value of individual choices is becoming new wisdom!
Collaborative efforts are replacing top-down control of autocrats,
These cooperative partnerships are now increasingly prevalent!

Once people seek to preserve their autonomous freedom to choose,
The old form of authoritarianism is threatened and is also loosened!
Respect of persons to work together in partnerships has more validity,
Then the deference to only the will of the few who are in authority.

Building Justice and Peace!

Contemporary strategy is built upon measures for "Justice-Building!"[26]
Because peace is unsustainable without provisions for just structures.
Structural violence that has been insidious and even institutionalized,
Is being addressed with models of fairness and justice as revitalized!

Unfortunately, the basic family level of interaction is still floundering,
Domestic violence and sexual abuse unfortunately are continuing.
Until families learn to resolve disputes nonviolently, trouble persists,
Conflict management strategies need attention as injuries still exist!
Economic hardships in the world economies are also a casual factor,
When families continue to struggle, abusers continue as violators!
Shelters for abused families are badly needed but are actually reactive,
Preventive education is essential to address this intimacy as positive.

---

[26] Middents, Gerald, 2001, <u>Crisis in Violence and Peace.</u>

Fewer persons are in abject poverty reduced to less than one billion,
    This is over half of what previously existed under a global pavilion.
When fewer people are starving, there are many positive side effects,
    Human health is improving with greater longevity as clear
    evidence!

It is not only due to better medical services to treat contagious
diseases,
    More preventive services increase the boundaries of human
    longevity!
There is now also less avoidable suffering than in previous millennia,
    These developments in our more positive qualities of life are
    historical!

Most of these improvements have been under girded by better
education,
    More women are educated as young girls with accompanying
    dividends.
Educated women are able to delay marriage plus have fewer children,
    Moreover, these women have healthier and better-educated
    offspring!

Men also benefit when women's education level rises to be
self-sustaining,
    The quality of living quarters, more nutritious food and health
    caring!
Men have often been the promulgators of both violence and also war,
    Women have been more likely the victims plus children with many
    scars.

Humanity is searching for more humane methods to settle disputes,
    Conflict management, negotiations plus peaceful religious
    concepts,
The human family searches for a more effective form of governance,
    Global issues increasingly demand that we formulate
    improvement.

Human Contradictions

Historical civilizations formalize deeply formed cultural practices,
These are often grounded in environments affecting human lives!
Moreover, family values and cultural religions are also influential,
When these are formally codified, schooling transmits these values!

Have you ever reflected about your family and community behaviors?
Are they reasoned out with consideration of causes and also effects?
People may be puzzled when examining why people engage in practices!
These are the way we do it in our community may not be questioned.

Consider the life cycle practices from birth of children until death:
Family constellations celebrate in formalized traditions of initiation,
Rites of recognizing the inclusion of a new infant plus rites of passage!
Training patterns plus valued skills are ingrained in these rituals!

Moreover, gender roles are also rigidly defined and also practiced!
Unwritten codes of conduct govern many behaviors that are observed!
Courting and marriage are also customized in order to develop sexuality,
Dress codes, couple arrangements and dating are influenced traditionally.

When illnesses occur, there are typical types of concerns and support,
When tragedies happen, expressions of sympathy show in our efforts.
As death ensues, each community has patterns known for "doing it right!"
Burials and internment of the deceased body provides for certain rites!

More patterns are amenable to examinations as this is only suggestive,
    These practices are very significant in the cycles of our human lives.
Gender behavior develops to express both femininity and masculinity,
    Usually, laws re-enforce the value preferences show as informalities.

Violations of civilized behaviors are considered by practices and laws,
    Variations only have small ranges of tolerance or enforcement occurs.
When intolerable divergence from traditional practices become known,
    Both direct actions and informal sanctions may be readily imposed!

Violent forms of discipline evolve from family practices in civility,
    Schooling will usually reflect these traditions in some practicality.
Expected discipline has limited ranges of tolerance in these variations,
    Spankings, isolation and deterrence are combined in these traditions.

These family and community patterns are foundations of societies,
    Generations abide with these practices that are known as proprieties.
More organized levels of governance emerge plus formal structures,
    Governance in tribes and nations combine the best of these practices.

Civil and criminal laws reflect the blended themes of these traditions,
    Punishments are determined on the of retribution and revenge,
Restoration and expressions of these civilizations see as ideal values.
    Violent punishment is meted out by patterns thought appropriate.

Communities aspire to both peace and justice in their combinations,
    There may be contradictions, consistencies and even inconsistencies!
Fairness is a key factor in determining the appropriate practices,
    When this moral value is observed, the outcomes are seen as ethical!

Case Study I: Abusive Violence

Domestic and international violence are similar in numerous respects,
>   This chronic condition persists throughout human history and events.

Historical records reveal how members of families are still treated,
>   Even with enlightened knowledge these old violations are repeated.

Why do human beings resort to physical violence and emotional distress?
>   Why do physical power and also psychological control still possess us?

While advanced civilizations purport to recognize the role of equality,
>   Dominating relationships persist as major facets of our humanity!

Similar dynamics are present in both domestic and in global violence,
>   While the scale of family abuse is less, the dimensions are rampant.

International wars become inhumane in their scope and velocities,
>   While domestic violence continues in most of the civil communities.

From primitive clubs to nuclear weapons, humanity is threatened,
>   The whole earth is endangered by the destructive consequences.

Is this an inherent need for hierarchical dominance that is sexual?
>   Or is violence learned so that it is transmitted and generational?

Sociopathic behavior is characterized by violations of social codes,
>   Plus, the very bizarre outcomes of not re-learning from our mistakes!

Why does humanity have chronic problems in learning from the past?
>   Is eventual destruction inherent in our human nature that will last?

While most cultures and nations support ideals of peace and justice,
>   Plus reinforced by religious beliefs and also governmental practices.

Are we failing to transmit these high goals in our own laboratories?
  The human experiment is inconclusive with contemporary
  evidence.

Children are often treated like commodities and spouses as products,
  Enemies are annihilated in order to rule over their lands and
  peoples.
Will the human family learn to promote peace and justice building?
  Or will dominant control by utilizing force and power be lasting?

Even religious practices and legal codes have been very inadequate,
  These veneers primarily seem to be frosting on a deteriorating
  cake.
Concerted global efforts are essential to attain both peace and justice,
  Otherwise, human beings rely upon false dichotomies of good
  and evil.

These challenges are identified in bold relief as contrasts to consider,
  Otherwise, the tendency is to gloss over more effective
  alternatives.
Future generations are primarily dependent on the heritage we leave,
  Otherwise, posterity may continue the pathology in order to
  achieve.

Case Study II: Gays, Lesbians, Trans and Bi-Sexuals

In contemporary history, new developments are recently occurring,
  Traditional biases about sexual practices are changes in the
  "making!"
Old condemnations based upon cultural religions and laws are in flux,
  Major differences among generations contribute to considerable
  unrest.

Cultures in Africa and Asia are experiencing challenges to their stanches,
> Religious positions draw on rigidly narrow views and restricted practices!

Typically, the Biblical sources in Leviticus and Romans receive weight,
> Selective interpretations are used to proof-text unexamined positions.

Often males have also been more threatened and expressed in homophobias,
> Women are less biased views particularly mothers of gays and lesbians.

Throughout history these non-conventional practices have been suppressed,
> From overt physical punishments to social isolation they have persecuted.

Male-female sexual relations may be considered both evil and good,
> But persons engaging in same sex relations are often punished as evil.

The ambivalence in western cultures have been somewhat uncertain,
> Whether sexuality is basically endorsed or diverse practices ostracized.

Now genetic research challenges views that GLTBS is a personal choice,
> The perspective that sexual orientation and preferences is a decision.

Discoveries of significant genetic determination is becoming credible,
> So, the punitive view of choosing one's preference is very debatable!

Older generations hold views of those unaware of the biological studies,
> Younger generations predominantly are less likely to be so negative.

To younger persons, sexual orientation is much less their own concern,
> They are personal friends of various practices so then do not scorn.

More western militaries have now decided this is not official concern,
> These recent transitions are happening without particular alarm!
Many religious prohibitions continue to be more strictly promoted,
> So that contentious actions are dividing a number of denominations.

For example, in the 1970's explicit controversies were controversial,
> The debated restrictive views prompted much wasteful attention.
Ordaining leaders who are gay or lesbian has been very decisive,
> Only in recent years, has tolerance become a position more incisively.

Almost four decades have been preoccupied with these controversies,
> So that particular communities have become split through arguments!
This internal discord has gradually been more intelligently informed,
> But major religious bodies do not transform with rigidity maintained.

Scientific evidence continues discovering genetic loading is significant.
> Choice and personal decisions are limited in one's sexual orientation.
But people resist changing their traditional views even with evidence,
> Their cognitive dissonance has major difficulties in change of stance.

Once people believe particular viewpoints held by historical patterns,
> These new scientific discoveries are resisted, denied or ostracized.
But gradually more informed tolerance is slowly gaining acceptance,
> Within a few more generations, there will likely be less resistance.

Societal patterns about personal behaviors are enlightened gradually,
Inertia and long-professed beliefs are radically changed
reluctantly.
When long held and rigid dogma prevails, authoritarian views remain,
Enlightenment is an educational process that helps us to not
restrain.

The practices considered good and those seen as evil incur resistance
Hopefully humanity will become better informed and less
insistent.
Laws and legal justice have an inertia that has both pros and cons,
As true evidence is discovered, humanity want less ignorance!

Human history is rampant with excessive pride of autocratic leaders!
A number have dubiously allowed themselves to have divine
status!
This illustrates the vulnerable nature of humans to become almighty,
Enormous problems occur in families and corporations
internationally.

When the leadership of the military took action to be more tolerant,
This exemplified the intolerance of both society and also religions.
Scientific research had also provided substantial research findings,
So that contrary positions were then based upon outdated
evidence.

Provisional Observations

Authoritarian men and autocracies have incited numerous problems,
Chauvinistic men try to be heroic figures but now less a
phenomenon!
Old dictatorial leadership is currently challenged to be higher degree,
Educated populations demand more freedom along with
responsibility!

Will humanity on this earth preserve peace, justice and order ahead?
Major hurdles are being challenged with a pattern of advancements!

The seven billion people now on this planet also hope to be sustainable,
"Not Immortal, but Sustainable" is currently what is socially ethical!

Global and ethical responsibilities are the major challenges we face,
Rather than destructive competition we have just peace as a preface!

Rather than national rivalries and racial tensions there is more to address,
Until humanity develops just world order, we cannot be quiet or rest.

One world, one life time and limited opportunities now challenge us,
Humanity collaborating into partnerships is the next cooperative test.

Destructive behavior by nations, tribes and individuals is "old stuff!"
Hopeful possibilities are unfolding so that these potentially await us!

Educating women both reduces poverty plus promotes sustainability,
Humanity can foster democracies that will replace the old patriarchy.

When human beings are respected, humanity may become cooperative,
Good vs. Evil requires more intelligent honor in order to be positive.

The narrow dichotomy of Good vs. Evil can be considered out-of-date,
The accumulation of old historical wisdom overcomes being too late!

Human grasps are perpetual evolutions that unfold chronologically,
Contemporary analysis submits there is more to the rest of the story!

The human drama now is played upon the stage of the whole globe,
    Interdependence is evident in almost all international experiences.
All The World is a Stage[27] aptly describes this socio-drama interaction,
    So, are we all performing in a tragic drama of evil wars and
    conflicts?

Human affairs are historically influential on current and future actions,
    Violence practiced by controlling powers continues as a crass
    tradition.
Until humanity learned to resolve difference peacefully by doing
justice,
    Bullying adversaries and innocent people will remain very
    destructive.[28]

Could this be seen with insight as an unfolding of our human destiny?
    Where we act our own roles as individuals plus global
    simultaneously?
We create our scripts in each generation in this drama cosmologically,
    Future generations will inherit what we leave to our own posterity!

---

[27]   Shakespeare, William
[28]   Middents, G., 2004, BRIDGING FEAR AND PEACE: From Bullying to
Doing Justice.

K. EXCITEMENT IN SCIENCE AND FAITH

We are fortunate in 2012 that new books by leading scientists are being published,
> These are outstanding resources that can serve several key purposes as now printed.

Mr. g. by Prof. Alan Lightman, jointly appointed Professor of Physics and Literature,
> Previously had authored Einstein's Dreams to depict his Theory of General Relativity!

More recently, Prof. E.O. Wilson, the renowned Harvard Professor of Socio-Biology,
> Among his twenty books now authored another: The Social Conquest of the Earth!

Previously, his book on Consilience demonstrated his interdisciplinary capabilities,
> He is not only a natural scientist, but honors other religions and other disciplines.

These two major scientists complement each other in several closely related dimensions,
> Lightman, an authority on cosmology of the universes that enter human dominions.

While Wilson, is a widely acknowledged expert on vertebrate and invertebrate animals,
> He has a comprehensive new theory of "eusociality" that is exciting scientific fields.

While Lightman expresses his personal views as an atheist and agnostic about religion,
> Wilson adheres to his Christian commitment as a small minority among biologists!

One sees the macro-universe over decades of research of outer space and the cosmos,

The other has done over 50 years of research of the micro-universe of small entities.

Wilson explicitly re-affirms his affinity for his Christian Faith back to his childhood,
    Alan Lightman has become skeptical of proclamations of all other global religions.
They contrast viewpoints of the broader universe in contrast with micro-organisms,
    Both highly committed to scientific models of discovering truth by investigations.

Both reflex vast awareness of religious stories of creation, behaviors and destiny,
    Addressing these "ultimate concerns" with reverence, conviction and honesty.
They are together unusual gifts to our series of symposia on "Faith and Science,"
    Recognizing the valid importance of other disciplines dealing with relevance!

Wilson and Lightman are both candid about their professional and personal views,
    Thereby providing excellent models for these science, technology and human values.
Both of these current outstanding books are certainly worth reading and evaluating,
    As together, these different authorities share their deeply personal convictions.

Participants in the Symposia events can be encouraged to gain access to these books,
    These types of "take-home" assignments will enrich the young and also our elders!
If you take interest to examine either one, your cell-phone call can aid wider diversity,

When seminar leaders are identified to facilitate further study
and investigations.

The timely controversial issues these authors also express with their
excellent prose,
   Are timely gifts to humanity, to scientists, religions officials to
   engage us aroused!
Your feedback can be elaborated on back of this message with return
for evaluation,
   Your involvement is invited as a contributor to these dialogues
   and examination

EXPECTATIONS

He wanted baby boys to be killed!
Parallel to Pharaoh was worried!

HOPE

A people hoping for deliverance
   Prize a Deliverer's appearance!
Longing arrival of One hoped for
   The One Who is the Deliverer!

Preparing is essential to be ready!
   This "build-up" often is unsteady!
Waiting accumulates expectation
   Receiving a Provider of Salvation!

Limiting Advent to only four weeks
   May need more for those who seek!
Humans want time to be receptive
   To recognize God takes initiative!

God does not wait for our readiness!
As Jesus comes so we are blessed!
His Incarnating is likewise timeless
Not depending on our humanness!

RECEPTIVENESS

God is aware of our lack of preparing!
To be receptive to what He is sharing!
With His own Gracious Forgiveness
Plus, His Mercy and Loving Kindness!

Our response can include gratitude
Thankful that changes our attitude!
To love God with all of our heart
Plus, our soul and all our might!

By loving our enemies as ourselves,
Demonstrates God's Commandment
For which we prepare the meaning
As God Love is very significant!

God in Jesus gives us true meaning
Prompting our response for sharing!
Since God cares, we can be caring
Inspired to be ready in our preparing!

Faith Friends and Family
Know No Borders

The Earth has been divided since
the Peace of Westphalia!

Yes, there were tribes, empires and wanderers globally over.
Now does the arrogance of Western Europe rule the world?
No, divided nations are fighting economically for survival!

Why should the wars among European Provinces still exist?
The Westphalian Peace assumed nations that are distinct!
This settlement was never conceived as a model for the world,
Instead, boundaries were drawn and imposed on the globe!

Do languages mark out borders to be geographically fixed?
No, languages communicate between people who are mixed!
Do racial features determine human destiny on this earth?
No, 99.9% of genetic codes are shared throughout the world!

Do family ties? Or business ties? Or distinctive color divide?
Do Faith traditions observe borders in order to then survive?
When have friendships been determined by state boundaries?
When has commercial trade been limited only to countries?

Why Does Religious Faith Prevail?

Yes, do cultural traditions primarily grow beyond origins,
Historical roots from global regions have major influences!
Why have Shiites, Sunnis, Sophism and Mahedians grown?
Do national boundaries determine one's religious tradition?

Christian Faith denominations see the world to cultivate,
    Obviously, the Roman Catholics reach out into the earth!
Colonial powers took priests along to proselyte others,
    Cultural values including religions shared with brothers!

Values, languages, markets and religions have no boundaries!
    Each academic discipline thinks about its scope universally!
These conceived systems are assumed confinement to alone?
    Many faith traditions migrate with their own adherents!

Religious wars of the 17th century in Europe left a heritage,
    Their ownership of colonies exploited people as natives.
Ignoring Westphalian borders, they started to impose them,
    Dividing tribes into nations without respecting allegiances.

Nations and religions have made cultural traditions of faiths,
    The Orthodox Christians exemplify devotion to cultures.
While traditions may have home bases for the civil religions,
    Blending aggressive nationalism and also faith traditions!

"Divide and Conquer!"

National boundaries on tribal people are not unique!
    Military strategies have used the approach to find peace!
Denominational loyalties and diverse ideologies continue,
    Splitting communities, families and even tribal nations!

With "decisive devices," power is being widely exerted,
    Separating antagonistic ideologies to be disciplines!
Homogeneous adherents formulate their departments,
    These become silos and boxes without any windows!

Differentiation is a phenomenon that runs in wide cycles,
    Dividing into different parts is done when doing analysis!
Science and religion plus disciplines and nationalities,
    Now continue to encourage these separation strategies.

When specialization is extreme, people cannot converse!
Their separate lingo is code to assume they are smart!
Career fields have attained such very unique languages,
Group-speak is prevalent at the peak of estrangements.

Why analytical skills are helpful, this is half the process,
After taking components apart, then there are challenges!
Putting these distinct parts into functional beings occurs,
Requiring the essential strategies of integrative synthesis!

Boundaries become barriers that are difficult to be joined,
When analyses into separate components are very removed.
Wars about nationalism and analytical sciences do contribute,
Dividing into parts is so much easier than joining together!

Bridges over Barriers

Walls that separate are notorious difficult to find reconciliation,
Dividing into parts is easier than synthesizing back into holism!
Competitive thinking is essential to penetrate to puncture walls,
Building barriers is difficult but easier than restoring it Wholism!

"Dispute Resolution" and "Conflict Management" are two strategies,
Approaches requiring personal commitment to overcome edges.
Bridge Building requires basic trust that peace can overcome wars,
Bringing people with incipient conflicts can assist approximates!

Wars and disputes are much easier to start than to find peaceful end,
Human desires for power and control counters yielding to bends!
Peace Building is an entire strategy for warring cultures to develop,
Overcoming division requires patience to negotiate and restore!

Nonviolent strategies are essential to confront power and control,
Bullying among individuals and nations attracts greater
audiences.

Even being an audience who passively observes dreadful conflicts,
Withdrawing one's attention that can be a reward for addicts!

Enemies rarely seek reconciliation of differences to achieve peace,
Continuing to fight is a polar opposite for hostilities to decease.
Disciplines essential to nonviolence are demanding to possess,
Because traditional angry aggression needs to yield in this mess.

Seeking resolution to conflict is rewarding for intangible evidence,
Passions need management of all other efforts designing defeat!
Without determination and persistence, the conflicts will persist,
Being separately divided takes total energy to discover release!

Justice is essential to seriously consider and discover what is fair!
Fortunately, there are skills being developed to face this square.
Leaders negotiating just peace need to be recognized and rewarded,
They are miracle workers whose dedication eventually persists.

Peaceful Persistence

Dedicated involvements are essential for seven billion peacefully!
One-shot efforts so rarely are effective to establish nonviolence!
Breaking into pieces is much easier than putting pieces together,
To restore wholeness demands total dedication and commitment!

Dividers use divisions to discover how to "Separate and Divide!"
"Putting-back-to Wholeness" is considerably demanding asides!
We need more than the graduated distinctions few comprehend,
Beyond Peacemaking is Pieces into Peace or even Peace-building!

Investments into weapons and strategies to deal with conflict prevail,
Less dramatic strategies are not flashy for making persons wail!
Bringing global humanity together into united efforts for peace,
Plus, fair justice to resolve differences that so humanly persist!

When investments into just peace are equivalent to violent wars,
There are major challenges to transform human ideas to explore!
Rather than wars between nations, humanity benefits from peace,
Then human efforts will be fruitful so your "Tribe may Increase!"

FREEDOM EMERGING

Initially life formed from minerals!
These elements are known as chemicals!
In between were more billions of years
The universe developed into animals!
After millions of years into humanoids!

Animals developed into distinct species!
Governed by multiplying into creatures!
These inherited genes from predecessors!
As primitives they were governed by size
Largest physically dominated less powerful!

Any type of freedom had many limitations!
The smaller of a species had oppression!
Their destiny ruled by crude domination!
Behavior was physically determination
Cannibal practice likely had application!

Females typically were dominated by males!
A hierarchy controlled almost all females!
Their offspring emerged into these arenas!
When strength was lost by alpha males;
This new conqueror destined to prevail!

If males could not hunt for survival foods
They were dispensable to be devoured!
These primitive conditions prevailed!

Species could readily become devoured!
Genetic-social factors surely dominated!

Predecessors of <u>homo-sapiens</u> survived!
They combated animals and cold conditions;
Sheer physical endurance then dominated!
Intelligence developed with these ancients
Gradually emerging into social dominance!

Oppression of women and children prevailed!
Subordinate with exception to older males!
The hunters and gatherers for sustenance!
Evolutionary survival was an inheritance
Living forward depended on intelligence!

These humans like other species struggled
To produce survivors who also struggled!
As conditions did change, many perished
By example, their youngsters learned
To pass on skills that they had earned!

L. ANCIENT CIVILIZATIONS

Early civilizations struggled for survival!
The survivors learned from trial and error!
All benefit from these tough procedures!
Gradually evolving to pass to youngsters!
As early civilizations emerge to successors!

Yes, women and children were laborers;
Plus, non-dominant males as survivors!
Together they developed tribal behaviors!
By archaeology we learn of contributors!
Who were born, lived, worked as providers!

Hunters were key in these migrations
To follow game as hunter education!
Many eons were needed with dedication!
Our ancestors developed by progression
Descendants learned by selective evolution!

Safety was critical for their survival!
Leaders gained control of descendants!
They could demand utmost allegiance!
So that survivors became descendants!
We are indebted to this type of obedience!

Unfortunately, wars ensued to endure!
Tribes rarely knew if they were secure!
Warriors were needed even to suffer!
Their lives were lost to protect tribes;
This provided that members survived!

Ancient rules captured women and children!
Males were eradicated as an old practice!
These primitive guidelines are powerful;
So that warriors today find them useful!
But future eons need what is functional!

Currently, we know little of predecessors;
We are indebted to these as survivors!
We can recognize them as successors!
Our genes and environment are indebted
To these predecessors to be enlightened!

INTERMEDIATE PREDECESSORS

From hunters they became gatherers!
Eventually learning to be "agriculturers!"
To these generations we are successors!
By hunters and farmers were essential;
So that later generations had lives vital!

Yes, still women and children were controlled
They were smaller and not nearly as bold!
However, humanity to them is indebted!
As learning and knowledge was transmitted!
May these ancestors also be vitally realized!

Males prevailed with their domination!
Children were laborers as possessions.
The women engaged in plant production!
No longer nomadic life an only option
As communities settled into locations!

The poor were attached to the land!
Owners saw them as possessions!
Slavery held many as concessions!
Freedom was restricted on locations
Slaves may be held for expansion!

Safety was secondary to functions
Serving the will of those owners
Traded like merchandise for sale!

Security was dependent on value
Less than human in many venues!

When disposed for lacking in value,
Slaves may become beggars anew!
Depending upon human sympathy,
Surviving on determined destiny;
Animals and slaves were property!

Exploitation became very typical
Using their slaves as raw material!
Disposed of when no longer vital!
Animals may be treated better!
Traded as merchandise by seller!

Human value concepts were slim
Life was short and outlook dim!
Size and strength were valuable
Plus, skills that they were capable!
Their destiny depended upon owners!

Serfs in Servitude

Serfdom and slavery were similar;
Serfs more attached to agriculture.
There was very little human virtue!
They were obedient to be secure
Freedom limited and few endured!

Inequalities were obviously apparent;
The workers and wealthy aristocrats!
Social strata followed strict sequels!
Royalty ruled while subject served;
Levels of respect were differentiated!

Rural life was then predominant,
    Villages and cities prominent!
        Tribal loyalties were per-eminent!
    Kings had rivals who were enemies
Serfs and slaves became small armies!

Knighthood was a style of chivalry!
    Rival leaders used them readily!
        Knights influenced future destiny!
    The Royalty decided upon liberty
Subjects acquiesced their humanity!

Serfs and slaves lead by masters
    Masters were under commanders!
        These were guided by royal orders!
    Life then had a clear hierarchy;
Everyone was loyal to Monarchy!

These humans like other species struggled
    To produce survivors who also struggled!
        As conditions did change, many perished;
    By example, their youngsters learned;
To pass on skills that they had earned!

THERAPUETIC PERSPECTIVES

Holiday Seasons are very elating!
    We patiently hold on by waiting!
        This is time when we are expecting!
            Families and friends are gathering!

Children naturally wait impatiently!
    Teenagers act disinterested lately!
        Gifts are purchased commercially!
            Over-eating adds to be weighty!

This season of joy raises expectations!
Balancing the cold of winter season!
As warm hearts greet in relations!
Honoring others with presentations!

We focus on religious and cultural events!
These occasions may uplift our spirits!
Especially as we receive many gifts!
This season provides many reliefs!

UPPERS and DOWNERS

For some this experience is joyful;
For others may become "less full,"
Going from uppers to downers!
Joining from downers to uppers!

Others are facing some despair!
Wondering if anyone else cares!
Perhaps feeling trapped inside
Being held like being wrapped!

A person trapped in depression
May fall back in a regression!
Energy expended by elation!
Is stymied by a down recession!

Significant groups in a population,
Do not find personal connection!
May have lost a sense of elation,
Becoming loners void of relations!

Perhaps you already feel badly
Taking another direction quickly!

To discover the better way out
Finding a way to turn about!

Moving from downer to upwardly,
Can be helped by moving forward!
Turning direction may be hard
Additional factors may reward!

GAINING MOMENTUM

There can be helpful approaches
There are profession coaches!
Friends might not be sufficient
As trained persons are efficient!

Physicians can check you physically,
May provide medication carefully!
Wise Physicians make referrals
To those trained to do therapy!

Psychiatrists and Psychologists offer
Therapeutic service that are proper.
These approaches can be helpful
By being trained professionals!

A limited number of trained clergy,
Provide guidance and spirituality!
Effective combinations collaborate
By blending skills that cooperate!

Persistence is certainly essential
So, teamwork reaches full potential.
Family and friends can be supportive,
How to become our helpful relatives!

Group therapy is also effective
Sharing by being interactive!
Participants express involvement
That jointly can aid "resolvement!"

HOPE

Hope is not magical!
Hope is very hard to do!
Hope is not what you hold;
Hope helps by being bold!

"Hope alone is not enough!"
Positive thinking contributes!
Breaking up to become resolute!
Rather than downward pessimism!

But hope alone is not enough!
One needs to be personally tough!
Patiently moving ahead by each step!
Building momentum and more pep!

"Hope makes us more resilient!"
Coming back into the present!
Bouncing back and not be spent!
Making your life to be decent!

Patience and meditation may work
Regaining perspectives that help!
Engaging with friends and family
We gain perspectives readily!

LEARNING TO HOPE

Hope is learned early in life!
   Plus, trust from parents and mate!
      Hope propels us to pursue our goals!
         Building success to be like our models!

Hope is what motivates immigrants!
   Leaving family, coming to United States.
      Such a powerful force is very crucial
         To achieve success and potentials!

Hope is essential in most religions!
   Faith, hope and love support decisions![29]
      Hope in reaching the Promised Land![30]
         Reinforced by anticipation of Advent!

People do not quit by having hope!
   Hope's an ingredient how to cope!
      Without hope people may perish!
         Making hope what humans cherish!

Every day we will discover,
   What before was undercover!
      Even when we do not learn,
         Discoveries we do not earn.

      Our leaning is often exciting;
   Sometimes may be frightening,
But our awareness expands,
Like entering the new lands.

Establish your own findings,
   Then continue on writing.

---

[29] I Corinthians 13.

[30] Deuteronomy 6: 3,

This is a creative process;
    For you, it will be a success!

    May your own discoveries be great;
    Provide them your namesake.
You can be very proud of them;
You will remember them again!

REMEMBERING?

How are you doing?
    Are you down and sad?
      Are your happy or glad?
    These are questions?
Depend on perception!

Fortunately, people ask
    Quick, easy and also fast!
      Usually these are friendly,
    Almost asked superficially!
Asking how you feel really?

There are wide responses!
    Depends on circumstances!
      Should I be quick or shallow?
    How do I know this fellow?
Not wanting to be callow!

If a friend, then one thing.
    If a stranger, another thing!
      If a Doctor, something deeper!
    If Minister, more to consider!
If family, even more sincere!

SUPERFICIAL or SINCERE?

Are you happy or sad?
Are you wary or mad?
When can you say "Glad?"
Or share personal insights,
May there be some slights?

Often questions are greetings!
These conservations are fleeting!
A few really want to know feelings!
This depends who are meeting!
Is there time to do explaining?

Assessing these circumstances,
Is essential for your answers!
Is this just a quick hit and run?
Does the occasion call for fun?
Depends on what is the forum!

Can they handle sad depression?
Or close up with quick succession?
Who can really understand feelings?
Or confidences about these dealings?
Will they continue with more meeting?

Of course, many want to be happy!
They hesitate to want to feel sadly!
Happiness is personally subjective;
Not expecting one to be objective.
Prompting both to be reflective.

HAPPINESS

Many persons want to be happy!
However, life deals with reality!
Happy was for Greek Philosophy,
As well as dispositions in history!
While actual living is sad and happy!

What is a definition of happiness?
Satisfaction? Feelings? Readiness?
Understandably, people are hesitant
To share what might be discontent!
Is it right now, or future development?

Contrasted with feeling sadness,
Is one definition of happiness!
Is there depth to this readiness?
Most people value friendliness
Reserving truth with willingness!

Experiences vs. immediate responses
Are key contrasts with their performance.
People search for their own importance!
Hoping that they will have satisfaction
Rather than feeling sheer exhaustion!

MEANINGFUL PURPOSE

Deeper ideas involve purposefulness!
Plus, an inner self of meaningfulness!
People do want to feel usefulness!
Prompting avoidance of hopelessness;
Deeply desiring a sense of worthiness!

Engaging in challenges is essential
So that others see it is beneficial!
Investing our energy is then crucial
To be uplifting, important to others
As we consider our sisters and brothers!

As we review our lives in retrospect,
Often, we hope to treated with respect!
Helping the helpless is respectable,
As we assist them in becoming able!
It is timely in trying to be available.

Doing both treatment and prevention
Is important for us to give attention!
Band-aids can help in emergencies,
But long-run solutions cure crises!
Our efforts how we invest ourselves!

LET US GIVE THIS a TRY

Human have importance inherently!
Life is not fatal; It happens miraculously!
A human being is extremely complicated!
Life needs to be relationally recognized!
One's own very existence is to be prized!

Persons can live in blighted conditions
Hopefully they survive in these options.
Many discover meaning while suffering;
Particularly if they have socializing.
People helping people can be surprising!

It is helpful if people discover hope!
This ingredient helps them to cope!
So do not give up but be involved!

People help problems to be solved!
Naturally it is essential to be resolved!

Let us join together in helping out!
Even when we may have some doubt!
Optimism is better than pessimism
Thereby may we discover wisdom
Let us have a favorable disposition!

FATHOMING

What do we about fathoming?
It is related to understanding.
We need to do some probing!
In the processes of defining.

This becomes a depth process;
Fathoming requires us to digest.
Our brains may do this exploring;
In these procedures for learning.

We engage our brains in discovering;
This is demanded in our fathoming.
We engage in this as exciting;
Our lives will be growing.

Depth requires our fathoming
Parallel to deep water swimming.
Our brain will also require probing,
Similar to processes of composing!

Our brains will engage in stretching;
Even without our own knowing.
Now let us do our preparing;
In processes of expanding.

Yes, we will be "participling!"
With this new word we are using.
"Participling" is also very exciting;
Others may see this as stretching.

This is composed in poetry!
What you write is worthy.
Each line has meaning;
We are now composing.

Use time to contemplate;
Some ideas arise very late.
Have fun in your thinking;
Enjoy while you are writing.

PROBING

Yes, let us engage in deep probing;
This is a key strategy in composing.
It is time to engage in deepening;
In deep water, we are swimming!

We are not naturally like fish;
And fish are not at all like us!
We can learn from each other;
Fish could be our sister or brother!

Fish can help us to swim deeper!
We learn to become breathers.
This takes deep fathoming;
With fish, this is the thing.

Can we teach fish to sing??
It is for more than swimming.
Like us "SWIMMING in the RAIN,"
We all benefit as jointly we gain.

DISCOVERING

DISCOVERING is a key process;
It is crucial for our success!
Persons engage in this activity
This also helps to stay healthy!

Discovering just keeps us going;
Does it every have an ending?
It does not go to infinity;
We are limited as humanity.

But we do have an imagination;
This is not extendable to creation.
We do have faith as Christians;
We can believe in God's Heaven.

The Earth will have an ending;
As part of creation's recycling.
This is also known in Geology
Which we study scientifically.

Most look for what is new,
It must be "the thing" to do.
This is now being discovered
We can help how it is formed.

Yes, searching is helpful,
Finding it is wonderful!
This takes enormous energy,
Because it is then a discovery!

You will then be a discovered!
Do you want to be the owner?
This may require financing,
Also, major decision-making.

Are you ready to take risks?
Your competition may be brisk!
New findings are exciting,
While also very rewarding.

BEYOND OUR CURRENT DISCOVERIES

There is a great deal we do not know!
When will be God's next coming?
Will we enter a "Black Hole?"
How large is the Universe?

What are unknown pre-historic discoveries?
How could we establish permanent peace?
How we ever establish lasting justice?
Plus, what still our own blind spots?

Yes, our lives are very fragile;
We are all on unknown trials.
We need to keep on searching;
As the future is now unfolding.

May we make our contributions;
As we keep searching for solutions.
Our human lives face challenges,
As we daily deal with new trials!

Bibiliography

Ackerman, P., (editor) et.al., 2000, <u>A Force More Powerful,</u> plus videos on four continents.

Bond, Michael, Oct. 2014, "Everybody Say OMM!" <u>New Scientist.</u>

Erikson, Erik, (1993) <u>Gandhi's Search for Truth</u> and (1962) <u>Young Man Luther.</u>

Grier, Peter, December 26, 2011, "Wars grind on; but statistically, violence declines", <u>The Christian Science Monitor.</u>

Jung, Carl, 2014, <u>Collected Works,</u> Princeton University Press.

Lightman, A., <u>Mr. g</u>

Ibid., *The Social Conquest of the Earth!*

Ibid. Consilience

Middents, G., 2022, <u>IMAGINING,</u> iUniverse, Bloomington, Indiana, USA.

Morean, C.R., August 2015, "The Most Invasive Species of All," <u>Scientific American.</u>

Middents, G., 2022, <u>IMAGINING,</u> iUniverse, Bloomington, Indiana, USA.

Nuwer, Rachel, Oct, 2014, "The Next 1000 Years," <u>New Scientist.</u>

Obama, Barack's acceptance speech for his Nobel Prize for Peace.

Ibid., 2011, <u>Obama on the Couch: Inside the Mind of the President</u>

Pinker, Steven, 2011, <u>The Better Angels of our Nature: Why Violence Has</u>
<u>Declined.</u>

Psalm 100, Luke 22: 17-18, Acts 24: 3 in <u>Bible.</u>

Research by University of California, Berkeley scientists! <u>Dallas Morning</u>
<u>News,</u> 12/31/2014

Rus, M., and Goldsmith, D., July 23-24, 2022, "We Don't need Astronauts
to Explore the Cosmos."

2022, <u>Wall Street Journal,</u> New York City.

Wilson, E.O. Extensive research on Ants Globally.

Author's Biography

Gerald "Jerry" Middents' has had wide experiences after serving as a US Air Force Captain. He became a Presbyterian Minister and earned a Ph.D. He served on the faculty of Austin College where he became Professor Emeritus of Psychology.

Invitations came to teach at Universities in India, China, Poland and Slovenia. He taught at Mahatma Gandhi U. primarily at Union Christian College. Then he was invited to fill the Endowed UNESCO Peace Chair at Manipal University. Lecture invitations came from University of Texas at Dallas, Ljubljana U., Mangalore U., St. Paul College, five medical schools, six seminaries and several community colleges.

He provided programs at the World Congress of Organizational Development Institute in Nepal, Slovenia, and Mexico plus taught courses in Stockholm and Switzerland. He has published seven poetry books plus journal articles, two professional books and a novel. Creativity is his special interest plus peace and justice.

Printed in the United States
by Baker & Taylor Publisher Services